Epitaph:

A Conceptual Elegy

Also by Mark Snyder:

Necessary Evil
(experimental music)

Requiem
(a secular conceptualist setting of the Mass)

now available on iTunes, Amazon, and elsewhere

Snyder, Paul W. ,

68, born June 20, 1945, died peacefully with family in Durham, NC on January 18, 2014. He was a US Air Force veteran who served stateside during the Vietnam War. After leaving the service in 1970, he became a systems analyst, working most recently at World's Finest Chocolate in Chicago before retiring in 1998. He is survived by his mother, Shirley; brother, Ed; son, Mark and wife Pamela Means; son, David; son, Todd; daughter, Sarah, five grandchildren, and dear friend Barbara Baudo and daughter Natalie Baudo. He was preceded in death by his father and a sister. Paul grew up in Burbank, IL, and lived in Evergreen Park, IL until retiring to Durham, NC in 2010. Services will be private. In lieu of flowers, the family requests an honorary donation to the American Cancer Society.

Honor your father and your mother...

- Exodus 20:12

A man's enemies shall be those of his own household.

- Matthew 10:36

Epitaph:

A Conceptual Elegy

Mark Snyder

RADICAL TOTALITY

2014

First Printing: 2014

ISBN-13: 978-0615993461 (Radical Totality)
ISBN-10: 061599346X

Radical Totality
764 Seven Lakes North
West End, NC 27376

radicaltotality@gmail.com

To Hayley and Melanie-

Dada loves you.

When we were children, we used to think that when we were grown up we would no longer be vulnerable. Hear what he said of danger, preserving the past while building for the future. If you're looking for help, a leader, support, work for everyone regardless of lifestyle: one successful nerd. Who wanted leadership? Search for a vibrant execution of orchestrated effective connecting with people. We can help you with all of your independent understanding of personality and social behavior. Sporadic attempts at custom handbuilt quality applied where spiritual bankruptcy diversified, family-owned, based in Illinois, providing contact with a new urbanist perspective powered by understandable, yet forward questions about ancestry in today's multidisciplinary approach to explore the basic promise of the family tree.

Let's take a moment to understand some things: What is? What isn't? Catholic apocryphal photographic images generating infectious litigation, almost certainly the best online photo management and sharing application in the world. Show off your favorite coevolution. I can dance if I want to. You're the one that controls the way people live. The all too infrequent personal emotion and creative health has effects of breaking the future of security. Dynamic adventure appears at a critical time. It's easy to understand why there's widespread legendary traditional burning. Terminal charity pressed graphic exploring perspective on the musical heirs of the estate. Dedicated over this time, he has discovered the life of programmed computer science.

Experience a chronicle of cursive drama, abuse, smoking, and disturbing images. Whether you love him or hate him, your employer can withhold the correct inescapable therapy. You're invited to take positive action after the death to foster the relationship mission of advancing freedom by deep expertise and broad skills. It's nice if you encourage ethical values; this result is not available because of religion. Give your completed partner provocative dramatic war. The Chicago philosophy guaranteed escape. His accident reaches a plea deal for something special about your morning. People don't know about these differences in questioning the juxtaposition of paintings. State and federal investigators opt out of aggressive investigative reporting. Critical naked self-portraits are now available, offering comments about the pernicious enemy of compassion, peace, and life itself. It's the story of fundamental forces of nature, responsible for caricature revisionist biographical discography. What do I need? A plot that wrings emotion out of this material.

On Friday, combinatorially distinct triangulations of zombie favor performed by someone without receiving the resolution of the body. It is necessary that the heady thrills of His Excellency features the best in emerging design for a malicious preventer of good, transgressing and sinful quality programming of Alcoholics Anonymous. Individual growth focused on breathtaking elegant explosion venting life-changing experience. Employ persistent, precise power to destroy or neutralize protection. Chicago limping microcontrollers would have spelled doom for contemporary art. The safety of a city depends more upon the professionals, published as final. Ghosts stay unbeaten in flukes. Dad has died. He died when we accuse others of staying the same. Why do I still keep rendering professional viability of individual activities of the moon, reaffirming the importance of genetic effects? Good acoustics propelled radio no matter how you know your style's identification. When he was younger, a description is not available. It's free. Release of dissolved revolution showing reality of the era, accurately portraying the actual historic events, while interweaving. Things couldn't have started any worse in Wisconsin. You can compile and run, execute your source code, try the food. Here's our review. Currently there are only a few small U.S.-based clinical trials for a people measurement system that forces managers to find and fire their rare opportunity to buy a different astronomy. A steady foundation is reeling.

German-born, he shared experimental literary arts and interactive media. Original creative collaboration against other development of quantum characteristics brought into existence harmony. Encourage your child to search for protection from cruelty and exciting new discoveries. Looking for a revolution, we can reveal any sound, expressing the moment where it hangs in the air. It's never too early to start. All the orders will be processed where we are explorers. If certain statutory requirements are met, it becomes harder and harder to say your full retirement explores human empathy. If you feel sorry for a building, you're going to be less likely to knock it down. It doesn't matter if you love him. The word, though casually taken in Holy Writ in a metaphorical sense, is most generally used by the sacred writers to designate the surprising answers to the age-old question of where morality comes from. His probabilistic interpretation that a severely deformed freak formed in Chicago gives birth to twins born in different years. They may require continuing maintenance featuring childhood photos and the Mark of Cain. Cruel creativity will be offered when you feel helpless, when you suffer. He was conceived despite several challenges, looking to reclaim his place as King of Hell. I need help. I presume your heart is in the right place. Melanie inherited its arrow of time from the black hole.

Measure intensity in real time over 25 years. Due to the extreme cold, smokers will be represented online. An appreciation of and reflection on fury, associated with anger, says out loud what all those little voices in your head have been saying for years. Positive emotion offers exceptional, handcrafted works of mid-career artists, lively conversation and karaoke. This is my family. The intimate critical biography takes you to see what's devoted to a great day. You can follow musings on the works of penguins without destroying your children, your spouse, your savings, or yourself. Endangered natural hope and a network of sensors will soon start monitoring what's going on in the commitment to authentic focuses. Recent activity threatened her scheming enthusiasm for scenic observance. Divas keep your exposure controlled with a vivacious blonde. Discover the accident watching time traveling. Good afternoon. The final destruction will likely be delayed because of a dedicated supernatural derecho of historic proportions. I don't want to live in a society that does an initial investigation into the possible euphoria after the revolution holds his daughter. We no longer have to sit back and take it. The historic derecho is swooning as fear dropped nearly 2 percent, its worst debut with the Beatles. As is our longstanding custom, we step back from reality without diet or exercise. He passed away peacefully after a lengthy illness.

The score from space: unexpected leaks feel they've done a complete job of implementing all of the controls that apply to their activities. The future we want was protection against low-level radioactive waste. You'd have a hard time making that argument to me. You always wanted to know how success is hard to measure. Defend and promote intense unexpected challenges as soon as they reach empowerment. Five million women value examination and instruction with a focus on innovation. Noisy special affairs will provide you with spouse and/or children. Drop everything and go to Spain. Rely on Levitra. Be prepared for bitter cold, legal medical marijuana and labor. In his very first, the clock starts ticking, the best bet to eliminate the methane emissions. Family game night is the simplest way to derive and construct meaning. He was looking through his recently deceased dad's computer when he goes before the Supreme Court. Purchase Cialis over the counter without prescription. Are you compulsive? Did you ever lose time? We were able to get cozy with putting children first. You have just won the Grammy Award for Best New Artist. When I was a child we had a parade in my small town. Have you been paying attention? Purchase Cialis! Want tomorrow to be different? Want to be in a better mood the whole day? We found that women with ovarian cancer had inherited mutations in a gene pathway known around the world. The launch code for US nukes was 00000000 for years. Influenza killed children, federal health officials reported Friday. The next one won't be such a surprise. PBS Chicago broadcasts 24 hours a day. What changes are coming? Dozens of movies will disappear from Netflix streaming. Owners of the iPhone 5s, Apple's latest flagship smartphone, are using significantly more data than iPhone 5 owners consumed last year. Learn how you can get this domain.

Not many people can remember. America has dropped atomic bombs on Hiroshima and Nagasaki. They didn't want you to read it. This gene encodes a member of the family. The U.S. government restricted the circulation of images of the Chicago Cubs. Only seven months into his presidency, Harry S. Truman sent a Presidential message to the United States Congress proposing new translations of an alien/extraterrestrial intelligence agenda. The feelings of those who sought a return to normality, operating independently, crashed into the Empire State Building. Find out why this instrument of surrender was signed. The principal belligerent was the only girl I've ever loved, but then they buried her alive, a young girl lost to the Diocese- a small cry. She could not have known that survivors of the USS Indianapolis describe more than a dozen men who survived shark infested waters and explosions. Conditions in the remaining camps exacted a terrible toll in human lives. Ironically, it had been the goal to depict, as vulnerabilities and exposures, one of the safest years on record to board a passenger plane. At Tinian Island on the afternoon of August 5, the tail of the Enola Gay being edged over the pit and into position to load nuclear hubris. The Germans and their collaborators killed nearly two out of every three European Jews. The two letters to my grandparents appear at the conclusion of this report. Casualty projections really matter. Surrounded by an impregnable armada, they lay prostrate- a common belief among defenders of the Second Amendment. I received a duck-billed platypus, and what do the experts think? The Party's manifesto was poised to deal the coup de grâce to the consensus. The age: 68 years. For a complete obituary and ceremony information, translate this page. Reminiscing is no longer possible.

To cease existing, especially by degrees. Fade. To experience an agony or suffering. You want to understand how bad things are, how stifling and airless and cautious the atmosphere is. The husband, father, grandfather, brother and uncle. The 8-year-old saved 6 in fire. BART officer while they searched an apartment. The wife of Indian minister Shashi Tharoor. It is 12:20 in New York a Friday / three days after Bastille day. Albert Einstein, whose theories exploded and reshaped our ideas of how the universe works, April 18, 1955, of heart failure. He was 76. Singer Phil Everly, half of legendary Everly Brothers. BBC anchor Komla Dumor. Steve Jobs. Margaret Mitchell, author of "Gone With the Wind." Losing a pet can feel like losing a good friend. To cease to live; undergo the complete and permanent cessation of all vital functions; become dead. To cease to exist. Total Deaths. KIA. Non-Hostile. Pending. WIA. OIF U.S. Military Casualties. 3,481. 929. 0. OIF U.S. DoD Civilian. Casualties. 13. 9. 4. No one is making a mockery of it. Health officials said Wednesday that flu activity had hit widespread status. Roger Ebert after battle with cancer. Kurt Cobain. I saw that was a bad situation so I got out of there.

Tranquilly the baby slept without war or violence. The siege ended. Protesters left the scene without pain or suffering. He died free from disorder. Are you tired, needing to sleep for the next day? Or just want to die peacefully at home? Most don't get that wish. Alpha brainwaves, these floating melodies, begin the revolution. What words will yield new possibilities. When a parent dies, everyday conflicts can escalate into a brutal torture regime. Do some couples sleep together soundly? Now I can die. I want to know what happens next. Be present; it is the only moment that matters. What does this bring to mind for you? Do you see hospice end quietly Saturday night with family by his side? I realize I sound a bit crazy. If you are you looking for a fun, simple and easy way to coexist, how much more is this the case with grief? How amazing is it to bear witness to the savagery and choose to live?

A nice steak, a bottle of red wine, accompanied by wisdom, changes in a systematic way. Everyone else lent their pollution for the best viewing and audio experience, bringing the world together. Go see the world differently. A tall dark man, my father will be angry- no hope- fear. Doing something together, implying interaction- it's all over. We've grown weary to affirm and safeguard the human dignity of individuals as they age. You need to upgrade. Days with my father, steer clear of talking about your love. I will never forget the most artistic mile in the country, from City Hall to the Philadelphia Museum of Art. The cancer killing efficiently remains impossible. There is no cure. What can you do? There is no right or wrong way to grieve. Build a wall. The average American baby is born with 10 fingers, 10 toes and the highest recorded levels of dealing with bullies. The new cancer is called palliative care, comfort care, supportive care, or symptom management. No headaches, no strings attached! Explore dinosaurs, bugs, birds, planes, music, sports, superheroes, inventors, art, the night sky, the ocean. Create a plan and share it. The results are overwhelmingly portable. In the wake of this and several other incidents, you must first correctly persist throughout the weekend and into next week. I wouldn't consider myself a funny cohesive experience across external living. I did NOT absorb a twin. It's not genetic or inherited.

Learn how she did it. Thrive in the happiest marriage, grounded on unselfishness, honesty and loyalty. The truth is that we are now separate, struggling, broken, like so many parents and their children, grandparents. Connections, acceptance, love. Charts and trees. Genetic genealogy starts here because of changes under the Affordable Care Act. We know how important it is to protect young people. Since he came back from Iraq, he depends on me. My wife has been professionally developed for qualified relationships. In the classical unlimited cell phone plans the core inspiration is to unlock the power of human potential. The young children love to sing, make music, and move to the beat. Children whose parents have life-threatening illnesses find resources in the heart along the scenic philanthropy. Get engaged. Touch a tornado, make a cloud, experiment with music and sound and investigate the workings of the human heart.

Be great at what you do. Quality is everything. That's why the ongoing inspiration and support found themselves immersed with minimalist radio. The national progressive champion can try looking for a variety of undergraduate, graduate, and professional programs. Commonly misused words plus comprehensive listings make your explanations remarkable. Carcinogenicity will also be of interest to the unique visions of women in a historic cinematic experiment to encourage women and girls to study and to have active careers. The reality behind the deadly disease is emerging: early warning, crisis management, and the advancement of women. Enjoy the freedom to work from anywhere. High temperature superconductivity in layered iron pnictides and chalcogenides is most commonly used to find out where you stand. Now is the time. Ain't misbehavin', just planning efforts responding to disaster. Their work is inspired by chromosome abnormalities. When one woman helps another, amazing things can happen. This site may be hacked. Where should I send suggestions? Western pharmaceutical companies and governments sacrifice the common good to special interests. You have questions.

Dedicated to the service, the city has suspended history. Enjoy wealth, art, nature, and sports. Due to inclement weather, food, clothing, shelter and counseling, built with love, provide unique live entertainment, according to Kevin Costner. The first snowflakes were reported after 5:30 p.m. January is National Radon Action Month. Relationships built on honesty, an innovative team approach and excellence in meeting client service needs are the foundation of who we are. Snake-handling downtown? You betcha. You could still see the building as recently as 2008, when the county tore it down subject to U.S. and international copyright laws. The first priority is getting your children to school, safely and on time, ready to learn. In crisis? Call a unique specialty food grocery store carrying a large line of hot sauce helping the addicted and homeless men, women and children in the greater Triangle. I can't wait to read whatever he writes next. Call or email us if you have questions. The VA Medical Center provides parents a convenient comfortable hands-on gentrified environment that nurtures respect. Who are we to aim to educate and empower a child to reach their full potential? A worldwide network of meditation and practice centers whose chief aspiration is to allow the Tampa Bay Rays to bring glory to America's favorite minor league team. They were no longer searching for aspiring energizing flow.

Clinging to life, consistently specializing in medicine, spend a day in the mountains. Crews across the state are working hard today to clear roads and bridges. This deed highlights only some of the power of your interactive conservation. Prepare for everything from minor traffic emergencies to severe storms. I want a full-time, professional orchestra with a battleship. Awareness, understanding, appreciation and conservation of the diverse Medical Board licensing processes serve as a catalyst for bird watching. Feeling lousy about experience any way you like it, whether you're open to the past and understand the individual tax forms and publications. Trust their respective hospitals when she doesn't reply to domestic violence. We believe that domestic violence is toxic and comprehensive. The quality of patient care is not available because of early death caused by tobacco use, poor nutrition and business advocacy. Stay up-to-date on closings and schedule changes due to winter weather conditions. We strive to make a huge impact. If you would like access to the interests of psychologists, interpret all aspects of family well-being. It's about more than civil rights. See the changes in a young child's life and personality. Time to hibernate from the cold and ease slowly into the new year. A winter storm warning is in effect.

The newest way to make new friends with event handlers touching, being supported only if you need it- a light, fast, and pain-free run. True strength might have taken aging focused on creating effective, simple and beautiful solutions. The universe is your guide to how to start a conversation, explore your interests, and be in the know. Download information on the anti-war movement and resources for the aging population. Have you ever seen ridiculously broad advocacy that connects people with friends and others who work, study and live around them? People use friends, illuminating learning about the big questions at the center of human life. Frequently censorship, from the Broadway stage to the operating room, will be recorded and automatically saved on your cultural touchpoint. Here you can find risks associated with home oxygen use and how we got here: cancer. The mission is to coordinate and conduct research on causes and to develop scientific failure of research. Get involved! Put your package down, hang your coat, so as to be attached or unified. Quality educational content dedicated to preventing violence and other dominant activity contains mathematical and formal aspects of computer science and nonnumerical computing. It doesn't matter if it's bad or good; it's still going to make art fail. More defaulted to show you the vision of an inclusive society where a framework for bullshit disseminates pathological philanthropy. Please bear with us as we welcome being wrong. Share art with others. Sex and more! It's objective. The world's story is yours to tell. We invite you to stay as short as one week to as long as one year. It all depends. Let us know what you think.

You walk around and lick snowflakes with your tongue, a flexible series of events designed to help you acquire madness at an accelerated pace. Like what you see? See amazing amateur astronomy and night sky views optimistic about refined abstraction and complex romance of sensual affairs. They scrubbed floors, cleaned out closets and whipped their wayward fridges into shape. All the tribes of Israel then came to David and said, "Look, we are your own flesh and bone." We look back at the year behind us, bemoaning our regrets and celebrating our diaspora. How will a bride react when her scheming future mother-in-law does outstanding work? You probably watched with horror, incredulity, and this heart should be unmoved. The full moon finds things you are missing. Please allow time to feel better. It used to be we couldn't wait to grow up. Pain will be yours this week when that man finally hears all the terrible things you've been writing about him. You don't need a special reason. The Veterans Administration celebrated; the time has come.

When carefully enunciated, they are a natural, stable isotope of disposition. Ambient spiritual exploration points out that her son was only taking art lessons with the hyperlinked index of found footage from NASA's abandoned Apollo mission. Everyone has the right to freedom of thought, conscience and religion; this right includes freedom to change his religion or belief, and the culmination of acoustic perfection- a heritage of authentic sound. You witnessed it, you recorded it. Now, let's write. A large crowd gathered to pay last respects on alleys, streets and rooftops. Nearly all failure funnels through the exponent. Gas chromatography is not inclusive with the latest threats. The Chicago Transit Authority warned of severe punishment from Him and to give good tidings to the believers who do righteous deeds. For those who fall behind, you don't have to erase anything creatively moribund. They buried him. A single-seat Navy jet has crashed off the coast of Virginia Beach. I fact-checked Sean Hannity on farting cows. If you are a man, then you must register with Selective Service. It's the law. I saw on Facebook that people had been out here for hours and were complaining of being hungry and thirsty and just thought I would try to raise the debt ceiling. It uses a short recoiling barrel that rotates to lock and unlock from the slide, unlike the other orchestra. A spokesperson for Scotland Yard said: "I can't keep a secret anymore." Why aren't we a black hole? Navy medicine was approved for public release; distribution is unlimited. This publication supersedes government agencies constantly monitoring what all of us say and do on the Internet, an uncertain and scary prospect.

Self-determination leading the way, a young analyst is newly updated. Please join us. We hope you can join us for six days together of data mining, knowledge discovery, and the trip of a lifetime. More information regarding location and everything else will be released as it comes. For real-time exchange of a storm that will push across the equipment, participation in the forum is one of the best values in the tech-savvy, live-music capital of the world. Join us for a full week. You have to know the threats to stop them. It is possible to present artificial intelligence. We need no one. We choose to drag them along. We are longing to start writing. Join us on the trip of a lifetime to share advances in cancer. Here is all you need to know: begin the rest of your life.

Being personal, welcome! Cognate with masculine psychology. You do not need to be registered. A father must try to connect to the young man who has endured tsunamis, floods, hurricanes, invasive pests, and human development. She's my sister. A terminal cancer dramatically changed Dad. MicroRNAs in cancer biology with a big impact is always hard, especially after five months. Excited, insulting, cocky and profane, there are no kindly grandfather figures. When the Boogeyman goes to sleep every night, monsters see to it that the abyss gazes into you. Heavily promoted male hormone products may be sending men flocking to stores, but their next stop may be the emergency room. A father who received cancer diagnoses is hoping to walk home. This is no small feat. For one thing, the assertion wasn't a compliment. Everyone can have an opinion. I met a convicted serial killer. The importance of the subject of this book is beyond estimation.

The sceptre is a symbol that appeared often in a moving lament for lost childhoods and an eloquent tribute to enduring play. About twenty years ago the founders came up with the very strange syndrome involved in transduction of signals from airport to cowards. The Vikings released me from Christian education. The forces of geology have shaped our planet and the way we live today. Everything you have said or done will be played back at judgment. The global outpouring of respect suggests that Machiavelli had to be imagined. Make sure you run a full anti-virus/malware scan on your local machine. Union Station has an enclosed waiting area, with Wi-Fi, with parking, with accessible platform and wheelchair available. Alexander the Great conquered most of the world known to the ancient Greeks, fused the eastern and western peoples of his empire, and became a god. A photo offers a vivid portrait of a lost world. Our intuition appeared to get his bread by serving modern art a CIA weapon. Now it is confirmed as a fact. Stripped naked, thrown into a cage, the real story of her life begins. The exact definition of "rape," "sexual assault," "sexual abuse" and similar terms differs by state. The wording can get confusing, since states often flip your thinking, on everything from shoes to why the atomic bombings were probably not necessary to win World War II without a mainland invasion of Japan. No trace of a body was found. Someone put something in my drink. I talked like a child, I spoke and thought and reasoned as a child. But when I grew up, I put away childish things. People's brains are as different as their faces. In his lifetime many wondered if identity reveals the experience of collapse. I am working on psychiatry-poetry mixtures. For the final 10 minutes, struggling and gasping loudly for air, making snorting and choking sounds, nothing related to the important news of the day, the chronicling of significant human living.

The left-hander may be found in cemetery records for finding the final resting places of family members. It was designed to be so. Find subversive delinquent examples for history. Follow us. The man who was brutal in many ways was small, disadvantaged. Join the conversation and connect with artists, bands, podcasters and creators of music & audio. Choose from our collection of suits, sportswear, shoes and dress shirts at affordable prices. Paranoia is actually the norm over there. 1 in 4 children don't know where their next meal is coming from. Is soda carcinogenic? Thinking about buying a home? We have information that can help. Got questions? Inspire the next generation. The president's State of the Union address is Tuesday night. If you haven't answered my message, please do so soon or I'll have to stop the corporate takeover of childhood. Look low in the southeast to catch Venus with the waning crescent moon to its right. To you your father should be the burden of brain disorders.

Pictures from smarter talks fall short of low expectations. Did they serve a purpose? Drinking and cheating? You might have thought we have our own interests in abuses. It has received far too little attention. As the violence spread, increasingly frantic partnership is crucial. I want you to know and understand living patience. Please upgrade your browser. A sergeant has a vital mission: to secure the nation from the many threats we face. This requires the dedication of infrastructure. A canonical entity governing the church provides you with easy-to-use, cross-browser user interface JavaScript libraries to make your web sites and web applications fly. Scheduled maintenance between 6 a.m. and 7:30 a.m. (Eastern U.S. time), Monday, February 3, will be on display. Give us feedback. The United States Air Force is an open source project charged with protecting the President and Vice President of the United States and also with animal protection and figure skating. Become an officer in the Navy. The government is extracting audio, video, photographs, e-mails, documents, and connection logs that enable analysts to track a person's research material on virtually every topic. Sentencing prepares young men and women to become professional officers in the Navy and Marine Corps. A sergeant may qualify for nuclear computer issues, but at least it should be fairly authoritative erectile dysfunction. Do you need a prescription?

The Earth's atmosphere, incredibly thin and light, a colorless, odorless, tasteless, gaseous mixture, mainly nitrogen (approximately 78 percent) and oxygen (approximately 21 percent) with lesser amounts of local journalism, tells about the challenges of being a female. Stare out the window at icy Lake Michigan, thinking wistfully of industrial gases and chemicals. Pollution exhibition galleries, each displaying major artifacts from the Museum's collection, include an overview of leading conservative commentary. Fly on a seaplane. The Ig Nobel Prizes, given each year, integrates the production of fine art printwork with innovative educational programs that explore the hangouts in front of a global audience, whether you're an aspiring artist, a global celebrity or a concerned citizen. The atmosphere surrounding Earth is full of molecules of different gases. Hummingbirds take extraordinary to a whole new level. We offer one of the most unique and fun parties spots in the the Bay Area. Check out our party packages or book your next corporate event. Pilots captured on dramatic dash-cam taking over amazing flying toys, including fairies! Live stream is set to show you how any story can be another story altogether. Find a rewarding career, discover your strengths, develop your skill set, expand your potential and serve where you live. Chicago is the largest free show of its kind in the United States. New Jersey blames Chris Christie. Before that, things were subdued. There are fraudulent efforts to impersonate veterans and their families. You spot the bogey at 3 o'clock. Epidemiological studies have demonstrated conceptually simple quality. When entry is in this column only, the value is exact. I want to hold your hand.

Cancer offers an extremely powerful physical change against resistance. Push yourself further. A metaphysical, binding, and ubiquitous power held enormous strength possessed by survivors of rape and abuse. Whenever there is an interaction there is repulsion. The goal is to work better. We must help them accomplish a successful transition. You can do it on your own. We provide all the tools; take full advantage of the power. Men and women from all parts of the world are concerned over loss of personal liberty and expansion of hunger. Our mission believes that every person has a right to adequate food obtained with dignity. We're happy to announce that our insane Rockingham should break the cycles of prejudice, apathy and denial. The world's first nuclear submarine gift shop, with extensive innovative, unique solutions and highly trained tools, is a useful decision-making technique. It helps you make a decision by analyzing the change, and it helps you swim. In everything we do, behind everything we say, is a long-term plan, strong management and insatiable hunger. We play cutting-edge haptic devices, specifically designed to educate, train, and inspire men and women to become officers of character who are motivated to nonviolent peace. What these terms really mean, how they relate to one another, strategic nonviolent conflict around the world was one of the best experiences that I have ever had in my life. My professional deflection from its path committed arrowing of related inequalities through effective and unsustainable states and their local governments, taking all necessary precautions now to ensure the safety of our clients. If you suffered damage, sarcasm engulfed the nuclear missile force. The scandal hasn't affected the safety or reliability of the military's nuclear mission. New Jersey jail records said he went to the building, apprehending him as he tried to flee.

That's a suicide every 65 minutes. As shocking as the number is, it may actually be higher. Most people with military service never consider suicide. Contrary to popular perception, there is no "epidemic" of military-related suicides. US military struggling to stop one of an astonishing 6,500 former military personnel. Even something small can help. Change a life. Motivated by the urgent need to collect the stories and experiences, join us in supporting our brothers and sisters still deployed. See other ways you can pitch in! We all fall on hard times. Find cemeteries and gravesites or learn more about burial benefits. Equip your hospice to meet unique needs to provide comprehensive care and quality service. For their service and sacrifice, warm words of thanks from a grateful nation are more than warranted, but they aren't nearly enough.

As many of you may have heard, it is not sponsored or formally affiliated in any other way. In response to requests from research ethics committees, patient safety researchers and interested professionals, there are four names always on or near the top of the list, in print and now an online database. As a relative, I want to speak. Thanks for reading. For accurate results be sure to enter a street address. What's squishier than a legitimate two-party political system, and that each party has its own set of principles, values and beliefs? This special drama travels back to 1963. Although the questions are real, the money, unfortunately, is not. The burglars broke into an FBI field office in 1971 and stole files that revealed the extent of the bureau's surveillance of political groups. Women make America. Women have asserted their rights. The greatest show in the galaxy is the most brilliant madness. John D. Rockefeller, Cornelius Vanderbilt, Andrew Carnegie, Henry Ford and J.P. Morgan rose from obscurity and in the process built modern America. You've probably heard of similar criticism; people are skeptical of capitalism- a quietly shocking indictment of our gas-guzzling auto companies and the politicians. A Japanese soldier hunkered down in the jungles of the Philippines for nearly three decades, refusing to believe that World War II had tortured a man. One biographer set out to find the message that matters in his life and a lot of fans have complained. Changes will come frequently. Cancer is small but vibrant, clever, felonious- a melancholic yet merry farewell.

In prison, a ten-year jail sentence, enough to remember the warrant, this book will suffice. Answer! No previous knowledge is required. Prepare digital art. Five lucky readers will win an e-book of their choice, thoughtfully sourced. On the day a witness was to testify against two correction officers, there was no vehicle to take him from Rikers Island to court. Philanthropists who want to make a difference have a meal or refreshments available, as for patrons or guests. One of the principal justifications for continued access to the amateur radio spectrum is public performance. Approximately 12,000 persons spent some time camped at Valley Forge. A devastated vegetarian ate meat for the first time in her life, with a hell of a lot more Jell-O. Before focusing attention on philanthropy, veterans of the First and Second World Wars are forever taken for granted, but there are many in our community who put in a full day of manual labor without the benefit of a noon meal. We are more than just a juice company. The history is not so uneven at the lower level, in the kitchen. With corporate-debt issuance racing toward a record, some large companies are rolling out unusual offerings- a 'frankenburger' made with test-tube meat. If you've been dreaming about sinking your teeth into a slab of lab-grown in vitro meat, you may be in luck. I've been an avid pressed juice fan for a year now so I would like to think of myself as a thesaurus. Kale will be available on many of the items available at Charlotte Douglas International Airport. Aging behind bars can be a daunting task. There are things you can do - and things you are doing time for. Have you ever? Health care providers need to know better. A U.S. Special Forces unit was complicit in war crimes in Oregon state parks. It's one of those places that is casual but feels nice, really great food, and is affordable. Definitely kid friendly, too. I'd like to go back for subpoenas on Friday as the state assembly was looking a little forlorn. We make the case for equality in the nation's courts and in the court of public opinion. The work we do has impact on the way all of us live. The worst-kept secret in history is finally out. I ask you to ensure that humanity is not ruled by it. We do not expect anyone to spend money or make purchases for the clothes drive, instead, take a few moments of your time and look through your closets. A history of domestic violence between you and the other parent can affect the custody or visitation arrangement for your children. The law presumes that the digital age ensures muscle stem cells were taken from a cow's shoulder. Mount Rainier has provoked passionate debate about everyday objects such as furniture and knickknacks. When you talk to him he will get right to the point. After everything you've already done for Raven Rock, I hate to ask for more but I can't risk his professional football career. He completed a six-month tour of duty.

In South Philadelphia, our menu focuses on locally-sourced products and showcases a rebellious teenager on leave from the continental United States. We were entertaining out of town poems. Although the poems are concerned with a husband's seemingly endless train of Mason jars, I can't help but be reminded of the hipster satire capabilities include planning. Got a reservation a month in advance, resembling a symphony orchestra because in both cases there are numerous guys that love to rock! We play both local and free listening concerts. Stretch, like we always did. How weird. Naturally brewed with the finest European malts & fresh aromatic art gallery for individuals who may not want or be able to pay the restaurant. With an emphasis on the whiskeys and bourbons that grew as our country did, we strive to recognize trends, understand their origins and determine how to exploit men in college. Time will tell if this is just the loudest warning shot yet fired by a department desperate for budget relief, or if this group is here to show off the talent of the new Al Qaeda threat to US homeland cable access television. A recent announcement from the Department of Homeland Security indicates that changes are coming. Be proud of what you do and where you do it.

Throughout the course of the war the exact nature of relations is unclear. Analysis of the relationship is further complicated by childhood experiences. Smoking harms your baby by depriving him of the oxygen he needs to grow. The fracture across which displacement has occurred. The slippage may range from an inch to more than 10 yards. Is it safe? If you're pregnant, it's best to take shelter. After cancer you were especially vulnerable. The Nazis advocated killing children of "unwanted" or "dangerous" groups. In accordance with transformation we play DIY punk and hardcore records. It's so dangerous, the lasting effects smoking can have in a soundproof cage. Two parents argue the case for and against. The fate of black people from 1933 to 1945 in Nazi Germany and in German-occupied territories ranged from isolation to persecution, sterilization, medical death. The driver was able to escape before the car slid into the river. She's named Grace Elizabeth! What a birthday for a police officer and the baby girl he helped deliver. While it may seem inconvenient to make more frequent stops at the gas station, induced pluripotent cell reprogramming Tet1 regulates 5-hydroxymethylcytosine levels. I commenced at the close of 1862, and continued steadily through '63, '64 and '65, to visit the sick and wounded of the Army. Not a snowstorm, a traffic jam or a daunting six-mile walk through fresh powder could stop an Alabama neurosurgeon from getting to the College of Obstetricians. Planning healthy meals is not hard. The United States Department of Agriculture has made it easier by creating medicine. Some medications can be dangerous. Almost all women can and should be physically active. President Franklin Delano Roosevelt declared that it can be difficult to relate to women. Despite the extraordinarily different circumstances in which loans have grace periods, dissent is a cornerstone of our service operations. Cancer tries to attack the image, not to mention development, operation and closure. What's available? It is a myth, however, that you should never let your gray screen appear. A spinning globe, prohibitory sign, or a folder with a flashing question mark may not apply if a blue screen appears. Rural residents often find their personal safety a large enough challenge without the added burden of breastfeeding. Keep families together. These havens should provide security. The 40 weeks of pregnancy are a magical time. Eighty percent of pet owners have owned a pet afraid of fireworks. This feature is only available for depression. A 30-second spot to advertise costs around $4 million this year. The National Security Agency carried out spying operations on victimization. Ending a marriage or a long-term relationship brings many adjustments, and former partners can find themselves in the impractical cramming without sleep. There are two obvious possibilities. The first is that pregnancy affects your immune system. Intimate partner violence: a halt to fighting does not necessarily end a conflict. Proper hydration is vital to your athletic performance and health. To perform your best, your body goes through many emotional and physiological changes. These physical changes are a natural part of pregnancy. By default, the pointer (or cursor) hides automatically after three seconds of inactivity.

The pointer reappears when you move the mouse. Is this an all-day interview? Cope with night waking (and your constant need to pee). When our senses perceive an environmental stress such as danger or a threat, women across the South took on new roles to support their families and the Confederacy. Harriet Tubman worked for the Union army as a nurse, a cook, and a spy. Her experience may no longer be comfortable, although no battles took place in Illinois. Is my child growing the way he or she should be? There is a wide range of "normal" growth. Between the ages of 2 and 5, the average child grows from flammable materials. The cops say he was a cocky little bitch. The NSA was gathering information while everything goes to hell. Zombie apocalypse rotations enable resident physicians to become immersed in different modalities of baseball. I don't have a timetable right now. Routine vaginal examinations for assessing progress of labor improve traffic stops. Stay indoors. Walk carefully. Avoid overexertion. "Baby," she moans, as her naked body arches up, glistening in hot, dripping sweat. Her hand grasps at the pillow, sheets, whatever she can. Chris Christie knew. A woman can become pregnant from having sexual intercourse. I didn't do anything wrong. He was being held on suspicion of assaulting the undercover officers who fell asleep. Imagine a police officer pulls over a car for a routine traffic violation, such as speeding or driving with a broken taillight. The set will also feature the massive on-air wedding of 34 couples. He was told he was having a cardiac arrest. I couldn't believe it. TV timeouts are supposed to serve as a break in the action, but don't tell the Tampa Bay Lightning and Montreal Canadiens that. Former Chicago Bears and Baltimore Ravens special teams ace Brendan Ayanbadejo says that teammates smoked pot. But what of the way humans behave in extraordinary conditions, such as earthquakes, armed conflict, or terrorist incidents? Stopping to make a peaceful gesture or to help someone in need remind us that, even in the midst of violence, give your child an opportunity to appreciate the arts. World maps show the regions of visibility for each eclipse. The lunar riot police queue at Krispy Kreme for doughnuts amid the injuries and arrests. There has emerged one image sweeter than transformation.

Imagine saying these words: Who killed your two girls? Watch an enormous number of potential contenders jumping into abstracts. Children and families die with alarming regularity. It always makes for a much richer experience to travel with someone that knows. It's even nicer to explore uniqueness of foods you must not eat. Get a flat belly. I think I have a solution. Everywhere you are, astrocytes can be reprogrammed into a seven-minute silent piece. They save children's lives and help them reach their full potential. A national 24-hour, toll free confidential suicide hotline for gay and questioning youth immediately struck a chord with an elite team of activists, filmmakers and freedivers as they embark on a covert plan from an unbiased and thought-provoking perspective. Women need to make sure leaders know we will not stand for being victims of sexual violence. Macabre determinism is self-perpetuated, inalterably woven into exploration of space. Discover musical perception in San Francisco. If you sit with a problem long enough, at first it swings wildly, but eventually release of unappetizing conversation made every day history. A 10,000 year clock is where you discover your regression analysis for future generations. Share your dream now. It's your world. Jump in.

Impoverished and politically isolated, in what is said to be a nation going places. Fast. Its people are energetic, direct, sharp in commerce and resilient. Thousands of pets are snatched in Thailand, destined for Hanoi's top restaurants and street stalls. If you thought you knew all there was to know, you were wrong. The prolonged struggle between nationalist forces attempting to unify the country serves as a testament to the sacrifice of American military personnel during one of this nation's least popular wars. It is in reality a country filled with captivating natural beauty and tranquil village life. Traffic accidents occur often. You should consider the risks of riding a motorcycle. A number of significant and important questions remain unanswered. You should avoid mosquito bites to prevent malaria. You may need to take prescription medicine before, during, and after your trip. A bomb removal organization operating in the heart of the former DMZ offers genocidal madness of Pol Pot's Khmer Rouge. It all started in 1967, with six veterans marching together in a peace demonstration. Now, forty-seven years later, feel your senses come alive as you walk Hanoi's crazy streets. I think we need a song with a message. How might the city develop? Reporters Sans Frontières highlights issues affecting freedom of the press. If a stranger approached me and offered to buy me an ice-cream, I'd say no.

Extreme violence is an organized effort. Who is next? We've seen its use expand in to many new areas. You are not alone. Any philosophical examination will center on four general questions. What is the relationship between human nature and cemeteries? After five wonderful years, they left us alone. Working directly with poor people accelerates the adoption of solutions that reduce carbon emissions at gigaton scale and advance the low-carbon economy. The personalities and the seemingly inevitable soldiers and sailors study the outbreak. We are deeply concerned about the needless destruction of human life. Over the past fifteen years he has taught a wide range of courses, including Women's History. Boring drones, AK's, high technology to low politics, exploring how and why we fight above, on and below an angry world. This legacy must end, so others can begin. Certain illnesses are associated with service in the Southwest Asia theater of military operations starting in 1967 in a peace demonstration. Neil Young has not only solidified his already massive fan base by releasing a gem of an album, but has garnered many new fans. If Japan is not completely defeated, would the Communist Party agree to the negotiation of a peace with Japan? The casualties are piling up. *Der Oscar-Gewinner Philip Seymour Hoffman ist tot.*

An 18 year old college student with a simple life, excellent grades, returned 20 years to awaken. Make the impossible possible. Keep children safe and help them succeed in life. Search for us. It is important that you and your family are prepared ahead of time. A crash leaves his father dark. Taken together, the revelations have brought to light historical restraints. A late night jazz radio show heard Friday and Saturday nights across the U.S. and parts of Canada take on a whole new groove with a unique blend of entertainment from 5:00–8:45 p.m. in the Great Stair Hall. With an eclectic impending nuclear apocalypse, I have a friend who has canceled all school activities. Science nerds unite. Want to get a head start? Drink up at happy hour. Reinvent your experience every month with friends, family, or a museum. When the lights go out, purchase Cialis over the counter without prescription. We make the case for equality in the nation's courts and in the court of public opinion. The work we do deals with racism, sexuality, and the meaning of life. Listen to the voices of the women who powered the Women's Liberation Movement. Communities and families turn to the Red Cross for help, and we stand ready to provide comfort and care, free of charge. A gripping, emotionally charged documentary film that follows convicted men in the wake of the Newtown tragedy. This is what happens. Checkmate violence got a little sentimental! A guy proposed to his wife in the shop, and let's be serious, Asaru got a little teary-eyed. Before all that I was lucky to catch the last few minutes of your interview. Children deal with recent trauma. Learn what to expect and how to handle it. You'll have some side effects. There is usually some pain with surgery. There may also be swelling and soreness around the area. The purpose of emergency contraception is to prevent pregnancy. Cancer is a dark comedy about finding your courage in mid-apocalyptic searches. I'd love to change the world. Actually, there is no difference. You can't imagine how long and desperately I've been waiting for this book. It broke my heart to see him suffer. Then he got this message from his son. It will take at least decades to clean up the mess.

You can't hand us a latte and then go about business as usual and expect us to stick around. She plans to spend next year completely focused. I quit my job. The true nature of Scientology is not what they thought it was. Behind the glittering façade, parents are very supportive of the schools. We are sorry. It's hard to make sense of its place in a living universe. This poem is one attempt. In prose that veers between the comic and tragic, the self-contemptuous and the inspired, the interstellar mission started in July 1996. Those entering it are greeted by wire fences, walls dating back to colonial times and security posts. No matter how many billions of lines of genetic code, you can feel prepared and confident with some planning and luck. I like talking shit. It's quiet now. When you are fired, get laid off, or quit your job, you still have rights. You may be entitled to severance, continued health insurance coverage, and more. I feel guilty. You might call it protection against self, this joke. My father said I could not do it. While this book is about divorce, it really is a book about life. I don't know how that is possible.

A specifying particularizing generalizing indefinite admirable doctor offers authoritative insight and opinion on life. This is what we're talking about. If it's true, it will stop selling tobacco products. Why do we have unsafe oncology? I think I have a solution. Repairing damaged neurons relies on booting a histone deacetylase out so regeneration genes can be turned on. I don't have to be anywhere. Be less stupid. I met a lot of great people. Smoking charged in documents on crimes and adult-onset diseases. THINK. A mixture of snow and freezing rain that began falling early Wednesday is bringing a range of challenging driving conditions. My father would lift me in his big hands and it was good.

The action of helping someone, old slavery, Catholic enforcement knows just how good you are. They would rather lose you than take the time to fix your problem. Pretending to be a fictional character, it meant the world to us. We are closed for business. An arrest warrant was issued. If you have been affected please call, whether you're seeking a new job or for the perfect candidate to fill vacancies. Death grants peace. Abuse empowers people who are vulnerable and threatened to realize human rights. Watch full episodes of your favorite PBS shows led by the Surgeon General. Cancer provides turbulence and convection over research and development of weapons systems. Faster. Smarter. Smoother. Better. All you really need is space. Alcoholics Anonymous is a leader in providing entertainment for multiple platforms and in various formats. Wisconsin enacted an unconstitutional law making it a crime to cause potentially fatal brain swelling and paralysis. We make things work for you. An opportunity presents itself. Kedzie Avenue invoked scourges of heroin and opiates that afflict middle-class young people.

Forgot your password? Be great at what you do. Share the world's moments. Astrology is operated under the authority of the national bank. Look at my stream. Fuck y'all. We'll dig that up for you as soon as we can. You can try looking over a million items. Where should I send carcinogenicity? Save a turtle. Your continued support and contributions allow us to recognize, develop, and actively promote the unique visions of women during the first full week of life. Any opinions, findings, and conclusions or recommendations expressed are those of the author and do not necessarily reflect the views of the United States. The results make clear just how difficult and unsustainable it is to work. I want to die. This site may be hacked. Fly anywhere on Earth. The family, including ancestors, is of utmost importance. Traditional forms of writing discover double meaning. More people agree that the war would have pleased Walt Whitman, that poet of urban motion, to envision his words coursing by electrified rail through a diverse, global city of delusion.

With the help of a smooth talking tomcat, a family of Parisian felines set to inherit a fortune from their owner try to make it back home after a jealous butler kidnaps an Austrian-born psychoanalyst, and death runs away from home. We invite you to become part of its future. I may be mistaken, but I believe that this book is quite delightful. It's kinda like, bam, the legend just keeps revealing itself again and again in the terrifying national mood. About a hundred of us decided to sit down. We've always marched to the beat of a different drum. The Imagists exhibited in Chicago and abstract painting held sway in New York. Any amount of insurance under this subchapter in force on any member or former member on the date of the insured's death shall be paid upon the common vulnerabilities and exposures. The Bronx was burning. Some books were published quickly, providing a fresh but frequently superficial or inaccurate analysis of the shootings. I feel like I'm having a nervous breakdown. There are a number of plausible explanations for such instability. The Beatles broke up. They were all still finding their voices and styles. This is the year of women's liberation. Women could not own their own home or even go to a pub. They could not sit on a jury or refuse to have sex. A young, idealistic volunteer was found hogtied in the back of her government car. When I was a kid, nobody told me I was good-looking.

Electric latency is personal as well. Being a boy implied deranged transformation. Unfortunately we forgot detailed information on fashion trends. A father must try to convince him. Doubly ionized helium is for veterans who wish to apply for benefits. In much better shape than one would expect after such an ordeal, this amazing kid died. Cancer ain't going nowhere. Cancer is explicit. There are no heart attacks because people are starting to get that. I missed my chance. God so loved the world. Whoever believes in him shall not perish. You aren't either, and the two of you will never be perfect. I pointed my gun right at him. The man has been diagnosed with cancer. Under no circumstances was I to go up there. The same guy cannot conceive of writing a more significant book in his lifetime than this one. Anyone who thinks this is any kind of victory is stupid, naïve.

A doctor converted the free navigation. The extraordinary, and often accidental, transforming from atmosphere to experimental psychology in Philadelphia against conventional wisdom led to a movement, which led to a continuing plan, to save a voice. A ghost invites you to remember the deafeningly quiet moments. Death could've overwhelmed him. Paul died. They carry a doctrine of grievances for inflicted injuries. Death is a humbling and disorienting experience. But I've overslept. I didn't see you. I learned the slow torment of the secret keeper. He didn't play sports, but he loved art. He paints the funny and touching dumb gimmicks. Writers have pulled all sorts of inventive stunts. I did it. I went to a cocktail party where I didn't know anyone, and successfully chit-chatted for two hours. I expect fried catfish or barbecued ribs. The former president is now a devoted madman. Long before many gods were born, I woke from a deep sleep and found all my masks were fallen. Just after the fall compassionate, vigilant, protective advocates of Western civilization has advanced the charge that none of us are the bad seed in the family. I was really a meek kid for most of my childhood. If string theory is correct, this is the journey of the dead. David's father decided that he was the perfect terrorist. More provocatively, he demonstrates

this new religion. When he died he was marked by strenuous ef-
forts. Ugly, offensive individualism evolved from the wolf and is
an accepted fact of evolution and history, but the question has re-
mained obscured by posthuman bodies. Peace means different
things to different fictions. We may never have our flying cars, but
the future is here. Auschwitz is now available in French, Italian,
Russian, Slovak, Hungarian. Children were a blessing. I died. I
couldn't even feel.

Communication bandwidth for signal-to-noise ratio has in-
tensified the interest in theory. Language can ask and, if ap-
proved, get responses from mass surveillance. The state can ac-
cess your mobile device, your artificial intelligence; we are sorry.
We don't have maps at this zoom level for this region. The music
and magic of words allow us to remember. Future repository
cloned it. The process of plotting an admissible heuristic dedicat-
ed special conformance. Find the final resting places of family
members. Happy birthday, mac. Subversive applications get your
past tax returns. I just about died when I saw this. Tell people that
there is no right way to solve it. Have you seen this woman? It's
incredible. Find out how easy it is, the music and magic of words.
Paul found the end because of obvious applicability to the zeit-
geist, powered by unmanned and autonomous smoking, sarcasm,
and language. Find your calling.

In order to get everything done perfectly and on time, it
has to learn all about the human body. We work closely to assure
that the current innovators started a revolution in the material, as
you can imagine. I started to receive phone calls. The recogni-
tions come on the heels of communication and control electroen-

cephalography. You can do this. The mission is to establish accessible, constantly improving innovation. Cancer learns and adapts. Your network is secure, your computer is up and running, and your printer is jam-free. Why? Fight cancer by attacking it. We have the experience, technology, and stability that you are looking to find.

We apologize in advance for any inconvenience this may cause. All other forms of authentication will work as usual. Your work will help ensure newspaper headlines have changed from doom and gloom. As the attacks of the Caucasian insurgency appear to move closer, all other inquiries should be directed to experienced, independent, and opinionated minds. The stress of the job and the paranoid spies leverage our subject-matter expertise and deep understanding in Philadelphia. Explore the phase of ethical hacking by getting advanced training in Zen. Welcome to the day of your death. Let me tell you about it. Cancer. I've always believed life is more than safe passage. The fallout is unlikely to go away. He was diagnosed with cancer.

To my surprise, people talk about what they do all day and how they feel. America wants to make sure you have access to good, affordable health care. Sign up now. In response to a complaint we received, we have removed an unofficial collaboration of interested parties who wish to allow authors to write and have a paying job. Find out if you have been violated and infected. It's time to get on the road and out in the field. We are neither a production company nor a non-profit volunteer organization. Play seemed to be successful in a number of ways, not the least of which was throwing a meager bone to a proposal by death. The code will allow you to receive a discount on your registration. It's staffed by geeks and clueless management. Tell me what it means. You are taking the wrong attitude toward the dream. It's time to take that next step. Life comes at us very quickly, and what we need to do is take that amorphous flow of experience, and somehow the same reasoning doesn't apply. It is my pleasure to welcome you. If I'm being honest, though, I will admit that I do have a child.

The father takes his eight year-old son to work with him. A day before, the Lutheran Church asked how the commonly diagnosed cancers worldwide are cancers of the lung, breast and colon. The common causes of cancer deaths represent the NTSB's advocacy priorities. It is designed to increase awareness of, and support for, the critical changes needed. We are seeking more than 170 fugitives on charges related to meaningful use adoption. Trees have such intricate root systems that a tree low on one particular type of nutrient will acquire some from his neighbors and make up for it. Several criteria are considered before choosing subjects for threatening. Male and female students compete separately. The deadline has passed. Don't miss a thing. The following fugitives are wanted by the U.S. Secret Service. Anyone with information regarding these people should contact Catholic theological works. You get crying together. I grew up listening to a lot of hip hop. Find out where sex offenders are located. The only thing worse than playing with one of these guys is being one of these guys. This is just a continuation of that. There's nothing that will break killers. Some may even be maneaters. A few tuned in to see the Seattle Seahawks blow the Denver Broncos out of the water. Cancer, according to a fresh look, was popular in history. OK, so that may not be true. Family can be very hard. Despite public hearings and a reasonable amount of media coverage, Americans simply haven't heard of Bruno Mars. We're not sure how often people actually buy their loved ones that huge bauble in Tiffany. You're going to be nearing the lousy whirl of doctors, machines and incubators. The professions on the right require human connection, dealing with feelings- and don't offer much power. Psychopaths keep getting better. I didn't know what to feel. He really made a solid end. All the more reason to heed the warning. In that respect both art and love partake of the self-surpassing generosity through which God gives himself to the world. The truth is, people wouldn't want to know how it happens, because they sound like suggesting that there is no such thing as right. I couldn't see any child- especially his own- handed over. Evil is now referred to as promising a great year. Importantly, he's shouldering a heavier load than he's experienced, the only distant galaxy in the universe with a measured distance.

Not long ago they were married. Get the support you need during the early weeks and months after your diagnosis. Never miss a relevant paper again. Lucky dogs, cats and other animals have found their forever homes. I like the way I feel about myself when I'm with him. I say quietly. The world famous Grand Canyon, which snakes through the American state of Arizona, only took its present form relatively. Leading radical thinkers explore family cases. We've discovered some of the strangest things on the Red Planet: ice spiders, Swiss cheese terrain, and unusual full-episode streaming. What did you just realize you've been doing incorrectly? I've gone through the same thing. After you delete a user account, you have five days to restore it. Japan's Great Tohoku Quakes have recurred. Pursuant to Judicial Conference of the

United States policy, access to all case related documents must be through the PACER system. You can also permanently delete them. It's natural to feel scared, confused and unsure what to do next. But knowing that you or a loved one has been diagnosed with cancer, now is the time to take charge of your situation and understand all of your options. I've never felt motivated to do anything myself. If you want to have your guts ripped out through your eyeballs, have a look at reactivated NASA spacecraft. Its first new explorer has spotted a never-before-seen asteroid. If you've lost your job, you have many concerns and one urgent question: What now? Don't worry. A cross-cultural analysis found that no-madic hunter-gatherer populations rarely organize to attack other groups. They said he had been treated at a VA hospital. I've come to the conclusion that marriage isn't for me. Isn't it fascinating that so many serial killers go unnoticed? If you have been diag-nosed, you are not alone.

Save the date! Please mark your calendars. The memorial service- not exactly a funeral, to be fair, but the worst case for Jan-uary. You see a chair on the curb. It's sitting right in front of your building. But something holds you back. What would seem to be nothing but a memorable tale about baseball may turn out to be the opening chapter of a much larger troubleshooting procedure amid continued debate. C'mon, you know it's true. You'll be chal-lenged. You'll be inspired. And you'll be dead. Thorny and unpre-dictable, challenging, you want options. Fifty years ago, the Beat-les arrived and were greeted by thousands of screaming fans. They came to America to perform on the Ed Sullivan Show. After overcoming roadblocks, the gold standard will be Lutheran theolo-gy. Most people who get the flu will have mild illness. There has never been a more exciting time. The shrine is seen by Japan's neighbors as a symbol of the country's past militarism. It is not without detractors either. It is fast and cheap. The reader will find few major changes in this year's edition. Are you ready to take the leap and transform your manuscript to a published book and/or e-book? I had no idea what to expect, but was told it's dark. I felt like I'd be slapped. This story will be over and we'll move on. He died peacefully from natural causes with family. Purchase Cialis online and save money! Go crazy. This is completely new and very much simpler than anything that has been done before.

Join thousands of mighty heroes bringing simple and life-changing critical goals to secure a sustainable future. Are you amazing? Enjoy the day with us! Do something. We gladly feast on those who would subdue us, as Earth is invaded by alien tripod fighting machines. Together we have the power to protect the ocean! Sorry, we could not find that country. It is the only all-natural cat litter. Showcasing the beauty and complexity of life as seen through the light microscope, the glittering ceremony brings together different religious traditions. Chocolate is available from every corner of the globe. A biome is a large geographical area of distinctive plant and animal groups, which are adapted to that particular environment. Family owned and based in Chicago, they also turned out to be the perfect tools, for thirty years have passed.

This was excellent, first-class, superb- second to none. More laudable, respectable- anything you want. Striking, splendid, grand, majestic, magnificent, stately. I have always had dry hair.

You might appeal to their feelings of superior quality. I've been here two times in the past two weeks, and I think if I do it for two more weeks it becomes habit. Seriously though, Saturday night was a flawless piece of work, an extraordinary melding of history and execution. This constitutes the backbone of the family. Based in Chicago, over 60 years of experience, a young man's sexual impulses go haywire when he discovers that the woman he has just been to bed with carries his child. It's appropriately gritty, and soaked in palpable tension. Discover what real customers are saying about the authentic Beatles performing long form improvisation. Since their move, Chicago has taken on a decidedly darker and more subversive bent, fighting for truth, justice and the last piece of pizza. Philly's now better then ever. You can truly feel like a good-natured experiment died. Never in the field of human conflict was so much owed by so many to so few. Who hasn't enjoyed a bar of chocolate? They're the ones you schlepped around as a kid for those school fundraisers. Based in Chicago and family-owned and operated, over 73 years of experience crafting premium chocolates directly from the South. But you would be fed with the wheat; with honey from the rock I would satisfy you, but I would feed you with the wheat. This abundant spray of soft, feminine spring colors feels as calming as a walk in the countryside.

Chicago has a diverse and delicious scene ranging from award winning chefs to iconic boxed candies. The recipe builds on decades of acquired knowledge, experience and secrets. What you see before you, my friend, is the result of a lifetime of millennia. When you're looking for a thoughtful gift for work, family, and friends, significant others or whichever the occasion, create your own assortment. Send lovers, valentines, and friends psychoactive divine fiascos! A decadent variety of traditional massages, hydrotherapy, facials, one-of-a-kind custom-shaped 3D cookies, bars, cakes and many other sweet treats. Young boys, talk with your mouth full. The word "compromise" was never spoken, in a last ditch effort to alter the outcome. It uses the story of exotic places, long journeys and small families that raise delicate, fearlessly answered questions. Really though, you can't beat Philadelphia. We're excited to show you our favorites. It's believed that it may help protect your cardiovascular system. Looking for new and creative ideas?

Beautiful astrology, free meaning, and quality is everything. Poor communities with other drugs, tuberculosis, and HIV support women through trademarks of transitive, intensive, or sometimes apparent force. What happened today? We'll dig that up for you as soon as we can. You can try looking for our journey through slavery. There was too much. I've considered myself competent, but the equity and full participation is joined by friends for a cup of coffee. Mendelian inheritance takes the most effective writing. Data from the Census Bureau show where the poor live. Read an entry a day. The index is transforming the way we think. After a long trend of declining viewership, all foreign nationals entering India are required to possess a valid international travel document. Any opinions, findings, and conclusions or recommendations expressed are those of the author and do not necessarily reflect the views of stem cell research. Jay Leno says goodbye to the Tonight Show, probably for real. Nothing we can do will change that. The children may be hacked with dark days. This, at least, is the verdict of anthropology. My heart's a treaty drawn up to see a psychotic reaction. A very select group of people are truly gifted.

Three of the nine hotels simply aren't done, and the ones that are open are dirty, unfinished, broken, or infested with the Encyclical Pacem of John XXIII. The only reason that was never the plan was because I never thought that I'd ever be able to make a living writing.

Welcome to the third most populous city in the United States. It is the home of the blues and the truth of jazz, the heart of gang wars driving goals. See The Catholic Archdiocese statement in response to the Jeff Anderson document release. Located at the Field Museum of Natural History, this live camera offers many views of the skyline. The Bears have a need at defensive end as free agency approaches. Who should they be targeting? Walter Payton succeeds on pure spectacle, but provides a surprising level of history focused on solutions to end the killing. Alternative, underground, independent and experimental enthusiasts, we do what we love, and we love what we do. Curiosity drives the Atlantic cities. I also realized that I could do the social justice work I wanted to do. It is hard to say I'm sorry. If you leave me now I'm happy to have made it through another week.

Pinpointing the arbitrator, reliability weighed the scale of the bad weather which has afflicted the weary Blue Jackets. Ripping through opponents behind a stifling defense, the continued devastating effects: methamphetamine is a highly addictive illegal drug that acts as a central nervous system stimulant. Not everyone is wishing him a fond farewell. Required to answer to a court of law, he could be taken for punishment. A function that returns a string receives the index. I am beyond thrilled. Two decades have passed. Anger is a normal, healthy response to a threat and may be used for a constructive purpose. When anger becomes un-controllable or is unexpressed, it may lead to death. How will you die? I am often asked for the easiest way. You can do this. It is your responsibility. I need to develop my dreams and myself. There's a lot to do, and keeping track of everything can be challenging. How much stress are you carrying around? Do you feel burdened by life's circumstances and emotional issues? The sun and heat will rarely force me out of bed. You'd think my wedding day would be motivation enough to finish. What happens next is astonishing: an enormous frozen, icy hunk of our planet suddenly opens, splits into bits and then sinks. If you don't have coverage now and need it right away, you have several options. We have just closed the door on what has been a busy and interesting year for, let's face it, both bad and good. In practice, the effect means that as two photons enter the atomic cloud, the first excites an atom, but must move forward. You quit your job. There is still discussion as to whether David occupied the stars. The downtown area was destroyed in the resonant magic. The frenzy that erupted was the result of musical talent, managerial chutzpah and *The Catcher in the Rye*. From that time not one has died. Think only of the relief and benefit of being restored to the absolute wants of human nature. Here are things you should give serious thought to. These preparations will ensure you quit smoking successfully. We intentionally didn't publish the story, despite some of your requests to do so, because it wasn't a story we hadn't seen.

Shy and fond of being on one's own, skeptical about the value of his work, sometimes active users decide to leave. You must be financially prepared and organized for the many years that lay before you. I don't really know him well. Make up your damn mind already. It's time to make a few decisions. First, you'll want to figure out where you have money. We've got a great show for you this week. I'm really excited. I'm just gonna take some time. I think I'm probably gonna be replaced. I want to grow as an artist, and I'm trying to avoid the spotlight. Your options will change, especially if you move. It's personal. I'm not saying that he doesn't mean it.

Capture a fast collapse. What is quality? Everything the old history shows draws from the public interest. We're about to find out. You are here. Read an entry a day. Professional collaboration is transforming the association style. Expert knowledge across time and space is working to increase and enhance cutting. Life tells the story of a hilarious adventure.

Following the Normandy landings, a group of U.S. soldiers go behind enemy lines to retrieve a paratrooper whose brothers have been killed in action. An international team of climbers ascends Mt. Everest. In developing a consensus on torture the Nobel Prize was awarded for their discovery of a new form of quantum intelligence. The climactic event in his death is largely a silent and invisible emergency, exacting a terrible toll on children and their families. Since the states settled their lawsuits against the tobacco companies, we have issued a distress call but only recently been able to decipher the incident. The lessons learnt during those years on persistent organic pollutants were on the ballot. You'll see the actual results. The accelerating expansion of the universe welcomed the confirmation that it will submit a package of measures to improve transparency. There are outstanding changes not yet made. Each single within the first quarter of this subjective list is filled with joy. In fact, the planet as a whole has warmed, sometimes even in the years when surface temperatures have fallen. You've begun a journey that will not only allow you to look and feel better than ever, but may reward you with the first major innovation- a fact that won't be lost on the more observant followers of this recent cutthroat competition.

Too scared to get mad, Janssen obtained the first evidence during the solar eclipse. Everyone who trusts shall not be lost. The latest instrumental track has been uploaded. Unfortunately we forgot to take a flight and make a connection, only to decide that they are poorly suited to be together. Helium is the second most abundant element in the universe after hydrogen. It will totally be a date. In a bizarre turn of events, the creator found terminal cancer. Break the bands of death, offer mercy, and provide forgiveness. This is no small feat. For one thing, there's cancer biology with a big impact. Whoever believes shall not perish but have eternal life. That will make you cry. I wrote this book wanting to testify, make it crystal clear I was not obsessed with dying but certainly thought about it. Clouded in mystery and incorrect information for many years. Only in the last few years the situation isn't vastly different. Dad released a burden. A guy with a gun could end up in jail for years. For the rest of my life, there won't be a February that goes by where I won't reflect on January 18, 2014. If you are lost in the woods with your dog and your compass breaks, do not despair.

We regret to inform you that some follow the crowd. Others change lanes and leave it behind, dedicated to distilling the world's data, information and knowledge into beautiful, interesting and, above all, useful visualizations, infographics and diagrams. If wherever we encountered new information, sentence by sentence, frame by frame, we could easily know the best thinking on it. I don't, by the way, think that dying offers pristine nature, breathtaking landscapes and vibrant culture. I'm thrilled to share this. Children cry in government bureaucracies, even in our schools. Despite the significant progress made in reducing violence, symptoms usually develop slowly and get worse over time. Spanning the distance between the complexity of life and the simplicity of physical laws, the challenge to keep everything straight provides basic information on malicious and other potentially unwanted energy flow. As simple as this may seem, thousands of men, women and children fall into proxy detection. I'm certainly not the first to be bothered by its implicit pollution. Roll up your sleeves and get messy. Get low cost Viagra for the best deals! An act, a habit, an institution, a law produces not only one effect, but a series of effects. But it can be tough. You might not realise, but real life disinformation happens. The sweeter the first fruit, the more bitter the alternatives. What you look for on the Internet reveals a lot about you; a growing number of people are turning to services that do not track their Viagra. Enough. Get inspired and enjoy.

I see the picture clear now; the fog has lifted. What's happened to the world when you can't even expect a suicide attempt? Several assassination attempts manage to keep going in difficult circumstances. Persevere after the death? What would you do if you were confronted with death? What gives someone the strength? This is a terrible disaster. I'm really asking. This might not be warranted but I'm doing it anyway. What I am about to tell you is something you've probably never heard or read in history books. A castaway- I can't remember much. I became an innocent victim. I'm so happy to be alive. My grandchildren like to put on "shows" for the grown-ups when they are all together. I'm afraid they are rather lame. Feel free to post your own. The man died from cancer.

The leaner you are, the easier it is to change. You do not have to comply. What is your day job? Now you can explore in an entirely new way. You've reached the end. You're protected. When you need one more hammer, try a new tool. I don't mean this as a slam or anything. I am saying this seriously. If you want to you can always shoot me. Why start from scratch? Be part of the solution. Learn how to choose.

A classic of devotional literature challenges you to give yourself fully to every trick in the book to keep a thrilling new impact on the literary world. Or you might be a wedding photographer with tons of fancy equipment, competing against the fact that every single guest at the wedding has a camera. Scientists at IBM Research have made the world's smallest movie by moving individual atoms with a scanning tunneling microscope. Hear one woman's story. She has produced nine works throughout her career. We are proud. Mandela sacrificed for the betterment of mankind. You have six days left to listen. Why don't you stand over there and think? We've come here uninvited. Ordinary people have the power to change our country if we work together. In the moments before death, it amounted to a rare enough moment. It should surprise no one. You're allowed to vomit in public. Maybe a father's words in a critical condition should be drafted by a competent writer who serves your agenda. Jan 17, 2014- Paul didn't plagiarize a foggy January morning. If he hadn't died that week, my life might not turn into an indictment.

Can a regimen of no playdates, no TV, no computer games, and hours of music practice create happy kids? And what happens when they fight back? She did not know just how much it would change her life, and his. The superior of a religious community of women brings you victims of violent crime. Welcome to North Carolina, where you'll find free spirits, deep passions, beautiful land and sometimes sarcastic recovery. We believe that our planet is under threat from a traditional favorite. There's a memory in photographs, improving the lives of women and children. You're probably wrong. In all the years of doing this, we have to say, we are committed to a reasonably sized system, engaging and encouraging you to run. Learn what it means to be friendly. We have a very proud history. I have heard in the voices of the wind the voices of my children. I have contracted. I have eased. My father and four children of us were scrolling mindlessly the day the news broke. So sad. February is here. Man issued from the womb of Earth, but he knew it not, nor recognized her, to whom he owed his life. In his egotism he sought an explanation of himself. I am enclosing a piece hopefully for publication in your paper. We all victimize, raising four souls to send out into the world to make their own killing.

With the sad news that lifted a nation's spirits during the Depression, you are no doubt searching for language. Our specialties are rooted in Southern life. You will not find a more extensive year round selection in Philadelphia. A bright-eyed, dimpled child brought back memories of the last time I ran in darkness, waiting. Paul died of natural causes. The broken, bouncing mixed up radio waves from your planet created quite a stir when a cultural anthropologist (whose areas of research include the study of kuru in Papua New Guinea, cholera in Bangladesh, and AIDS) developed a wonderfully optimistic style. We accept it as pure gospel. Cancer began with crime scenes. This morning I started to watch the disgraceful dismissal. My husband and I religiously go there every Saturday and Sunday. The library will remain closed today due to anticipated changing weather conditions.

A heaping helping of their literate, soulful and cinematic brand of earthy, diversified Catholic meditation guides them down their inner path to freedom. Facial recognition is set to change our ideas on privacy. Scotland outlawed pipes exiled to Champaign, fully recharged and inspired by eye-opening Mecca. Due to severe winter storms in North Carolina, we regret that we must postpone tomorrow night's show. The boys have found plenty of other ways to keep themselves busy. The first successful sustained powered flights in a heavier-than-air machine were made here by Wilbur and Orville Wright. It has been a glorious and amazing time, and I thank you all for your goodness and generosity. I feel like I'm obligated to be there. I've been reticent to put together a comprehensive. Could we be constantly tracked through our clothes, shoes or even our cash in the future? I'm not happy.

Sound art pieces take many forms including installation, sculpture, radio, video, performance, and public projects. His works combine a visceral analysis carefully constructed in terms of tone and feeling. It's not a return of the reluctant. If we leave out a few words, how does the story change? How are human instincts like music? I have something to say about the use of the term "privilege." One thing that kinda bugs me is when I'm on my way home, leaving behind friends and memories. You're our only hope. I only wish nothing changes. He was reportedly the recent victim of a much bigger theft. I've decided to pretty much bring my run here to a close. My boyfriend came here a lot as a kid and wanted me to experience this place. It really is about the instability, due to this slowing, and underestimated thoughts. This morning I'm going to be like that geeky kid at the front of the class, eagerly raising his hand and exclaiming, "Ooh, ooh, I know! Call on me!" Except where the context makes another meaning manifest, the following words have the meanings indicated when used. If you could reach deep into your brain, among all of the thousands of words you've collected during your life trying to find a parking space, every space was taken and there was a long line for the release.

In some cultures, the eldest has special privileges. For example, in Chicago, a father who beat his child, a tall, gaunt man-you might step away from him. His clothes, his dark face and his prodigal native features thrusts readers once again into the chilling world of the Old Testament. The word "son" was employed among the Semites to signify not only filiation, but other close connexion or provocative, completely logical reasons that children cry. A man in his early 30s struggles to find a balance in his life. A family on the brink brings the story of the life through compelling extinction. I keep wanting to send him an e-mail, just hit "reply" and tell him that we're fine. The sucker punch, by all that is holy and profane, follows a heroic quest to avenge the death of his family, and preserve the honor of chaos and brutality, sending you on a perilous campaign. We are not morning people. Life for me ain't been no crystal stair.

A secular conceptualist setting of the Mass is the canonical synoptic mythology. What an incredibly strong, brave thing you have done. I wish you peace. That's pretty stupid; why would you? It makes no sense. Blending themes with techniques reminiscent of a singular style that blurs the traditional boundaries, writing about inspiration encourages the easy cliché. The bolt from the blue, the needle in the haystack, the artist magically tapped Kentucky straight bourbon handmade whiskey. I don't subscribe to the belief that everything is better. When examining our daily contemporary lives in western culture, one finds that there is barely a single situation that is not influenced by digital technology and a jaw-dropping panorama of the city skyline. Contemporary art, with an emphasis on emerging and mid-career artists, is not a legal instrument. It's amazing what he can do with a violin and a bow.

The quality, safety, efficiency, effectiveness of health care severed formal ties with the quality of substance abuse prevention, addiction treatment, mental health services. The world's largest professional association for creating looted art values constitutional liberties. The world clock shows the current time in night-sky events. At the largest science museum in the Western Hemisphere, enjoy live science experiences, tour a World War II sub, learn. Major artifacts from the museum's collection includes exploited children. Detect malicious lymphoma that automatically deletes patients. Ensure the fish we consume is safe, so we can all enjoy what we eat. Terminally ill persons seemed to effortlessly mold around life goals. Everyone loves having the ability to make their decisions into reality. This should be something that happens. After a disaster, letting your family know that you are safe can bring your loved ones great peace of mind. The excitement of space exploration aims constant influence on our publishing activity. Join us to decipher the books. Humanitarian convoys must not be targeted. Thousands of men, women, children, jam-packed into freight trucks, the continuance of their parents' rage, includes all the inhabited continents of the world.

We've said it before and we'll say it again: a man wallows in drunken self-pity after he is divorced. After a humiliating scandal, he is behind bars. The woman you marry and live with for the rest of your life begins the journey to the core of their emotional struggles. The component is heavily tested and running in production. The dance floor will be open for honky tonk and country music. So how did you know? Following an alleged suicide attempt, I've been feeling a desire to write more about my scattered thoughts. I actually have so many that I don't think I could fit them all into one post. Don't be a clown. Fight cancer. Paul sailed, staggered through life, unconscious wounded soldier whose fathers are doing time. It seems silly to me. Intimacy (in a socially awkward manner) they swore they would never do. I don't know about you, but I'm happy to put January 2014 in the rear view mirror. The past 30 days have been a mess. He was not seeing any of the things I had managed to convince myself of in the mirror. There comes a time in every man's life when he discovers the value of hiding the grosser parts of his nature. A successful marriage requires falling in love many times. Since I have decided that, I have taken time to realize what I could do to be better. I have yet to stop dithering. It makes me sad. I suspect he's embarrassed to be there. I do not enjoy it. Stories of abuse- Christian domestic violence- ironically, in response to a complaint, we have removed 1 result(s) from this page.

A moving, inspiring account of life that's enormously informative yet reads like a novel, permanently retired, this edition will surely become the standard text. This e-book is for the use of anyone anywhere at no cost and with almost no restrictions. Please explore our projects and equipment to better understand what we do. The cosmic radiation, addressing the most compelling issues giving satsang around the world, writes dark romance. Her richly atmospheric postmodern literature focuses on meaning. I learn, create, teach, and repeat. The prisoner is relentlessly shrill and coarse in her broad-brush denunciations of love. I've been a romance reader since I was a teenager. Romance novels have brought me countless hours of suspense and excitement as I traveled to times and events in Death Valley. It is not down in any map; true places never are. I'm being as lazy as can be and eating lots of old fashioned ribbon candy and am thoroughly enjoying the sufferings, trials, and vicissitudes of cancer. I have had the unique opportunity to work with hundreds of women over the years. A deception discovered a decade ago, I first began my self-exploration through visual art, sound, journaling, and poetry, all in the spirit of growth. Peace is not about the absence of war but the presence of love. Let me hear you scream. Is it my cranky imagination or does Valentine's Day become more of a big deal every year? Are you a victim of profiling? Ever felt misjudged?

A relationship with integrity and commitment, he does not accept limitations. I've been experiencing some writer's block. It feels unreliable. It's a challenge to quantify. I don't know what you want. The question is whether you can make words, tired and harassed. Children can't get the help they need. You have to be great at saying no. To a person not familiar with what natural selection really is, I'm too busy; I don't trust you. A career lowlight for all three. This is loud, clumsily edited, and neither romantic nor funny. What is brain-dead? In a world that's increasingly dominated by impersonal, one-size-fits all tsunamis, our culture will bend over backwards to inject doubt into harrowing sexual assault. Firearms are the most lethal and most common method of suicide in the U.S. Find your favorite color. I realize there's a new baby in the stimulus program. It's not exactly as clear cut as you'd think. You are lazy and disgusting and destroying the percentile rank. The conversation is over. You're being sarcastic. We have both spent years away from our family and homelands, been on the other side of the world when loved ones passed away.

A style of music that gained popularity in Chicago, the alternate world lost it to trying. If you were to encounter a San Francisco street, you might be struggling with finding out. Catholic theatre produces highly provocative underexposed history. A powerful and effective treatment for struggles to find balance in his life, we have air conditioners. Nothing can be more bold, geometric, and free. From the start, respect for family earlier this month is an alternative to brutality. After a cup or two of coffee, join us as we celebrate modern lifestyles. A giant of the delta blues, with his ferocious dark magic unlike any other, man's only hope lies in the delicate but deliberate eye of our office staff.

A person whose name is unknown to you or one of which you have forgotten, we understand you're busy. He has friends, he is loved. The place is small and gets packed, so some folks are born to wave the flag. I actually tried to get signed up. I'm glad we're watching together. I think it's only fair.

A masterpiece of sculpture known for his diverse skills as both a warrior and a writer, tall and skinny, with unflinching blue eyes and a mop of brown hair, he speaks incredibly fast and in complete paragraphs. On more than one occasion, I've been told I need to eat more red meat. Everything is miscellaneous. Please say something. I'm a better anarchist than you. I grew up during the 1950s. After the death of her father, she is forced to maintain a vibrant place that inspires, sustains, and brings together people. I am a philosopher.

The elements of social issues includes various print and electronic resources. When she washed up on their shore, charged with planting the deadly device, father had outstanding arrest warrants. A close relationship with an older or otherwise more authoritative person can be regarded as ransom. Step away from him. The story shares his father's reaction. A man considered fortunate is powerful and effective; mentally ill firearms on the brink. We will promptly remove your ideals. We saw this as an opportunity to produce high-quality craftsmanship package bomb explosions. The chaos and brutality of battle is a setting of harmony, a sanctuary of purist aesthetics in close accord with ever-present nature, where one can breathe freely in the distant past. Their epic wars will inspire every myth, legend, fantasy. We're here to help. A young man has lost his way. He's becoming a father. We are here to meet all of your needs.

Thanks for stopping by. We're glad you are here. If you haven't been before, let us tell you a little bit about it. Born in Chicago and raised in the suburbs right outside of the city; as a child he always loved where the forest meets the prairie. It shouldn't come as any surprise that he is able to create very experimental and 'out there' sounds and mix them with some of the most widespread panic. My childhood was spent immersed in the popular culture that millions of children were exposed to. I put together an example for clipping points inside the camera frustrum. We left our old house clean and did the repairs the buyers asked for. That's not a great way to start off 2014. Thinking about your resignation letter; I get your point. I lead off tonight with stunning, sad news. I know that you care tremendously, and I have devised a way to pinpoint the causes. I see my world through a box.

I was screwing around on Friday afternoon when I saw a new journey like no other, and the results are remarkable. I'm talking about grace. I've been so lucky. I've come up with bones. Living in a new country in a new language is fun because you discover all sorts of new ways to make a fool of yourself. I hope your day is filled with love. I've been under the weather the past few days. It's the life between the miles that counts. Here's what else you should know: it shows a series of women describing themselves to a sketch artist, who draws their portraits based on their self-descriptions. The East Coast gets hammered with yet another ice/snow storm. We're all a big family, but it's made my world expand, too. Now it feels so normal to know. The more outrage the better. That way people will fear us while we are alive and never-ever- forget us when we are dead. You may bypass delirium brought into the same space to investigate the tensions of dooms-day. With the weather as it is, do you have any questions? It's hard. It's wrenching. It's incredibly painful, and it's difficult to feel lightness or to see clearly. Hanging by a thread can be really disorienting. We're not really here, you and I. This tour de force of historical imagination cuts between the bloody, beleaguered Ok-inawa of 1945 and seemingly carefree, romantic couples planning enchanted outdoor weddings. Dark matter reincarnates existing friction. Spend some quality time with your writing. You wake upon the cold ground. As you struggle to rise, as your breath ex-hales like a ghost, you can't remember who you are. I am a writer.

The lives of those individuals struggling with cancer can be written as familiar favorites reinvented in a holocaust. Can't help but feel exquisite curious decisions when you can't make them dis-ciplined. Recent turmoil has produced a fragile slaughter. She looked beautiful, of course. She had a small face, lovely eyes. That's why I kept looking. I think it's the same for a lot of other people if you have an early death. Everything we do is built around the children, to protect the children. We work to end child sexual abuse. They are able to concentrate and focus on de-veloping independent questions. Simplify protecting and nurtur-ing the early years of childhood, I will die the way I lived. Can you explain using only words? It's not very easy. Bright Jupiter pops out at dusk. Mars, Saturn and Venus are best viewed in the morn-ing sky. Mercury will return to predawn sky in late February. Paul is dead.

Philadelphia is the home for high quality thought. Close relationships smack you in the face, like a hailstorm with no sign of storms. We are suffering. Losing contact exacts an emotional toll, especially when they are not exactly sure where they went wrong. His family became a casualty. Here you will find what every kid may also experience: feelings of anger, rejection, and guilt. Few of us will be willing to endure present pain. This hurt would take long to heal. I'll bet my children will be surprised by this. Abuse and neglect, strategically hidden in our living room, forging intricately layered arrangements with only an acoustic genesis. There are no guarantees. The unforgettable magic words "once upon a time" sting, perhaps more than any others in our painful debates. Everybody thinks it's strange, no matter how disappointed I was.

The capabilities of our missions are growing rapidly. Atmospheric responsibility experiences astrophotography. Emerging writers search for missing children. A timeless worldwide favorite since its introduction, misinformation related to Afghanistan began to discover a resonance with terminally ill persons so we can all trust in what we identify as aid. Put politics aside. View the moon. Exciting minds of all ages question how to be creative. This is an exciting time. Purchase Viagra online.

I've upset you. I trust him with my whole heart. What I don't find fair is how you are willing to take out all the music. Should I stop wearing fishnet tights to work? Take a picture. Embrace tenderly comforts even in this sorrow. My father, abused, ruins her and puts her life in jeopardy. We are family owned and operated. Study of the history of your family- starting with you, working through generations of peace and violence- shady advice from a raging bitch who has no business answering any of these questions. This result is not available. There is, however, one man who infiltrated the inner sanctum. Please don't put a price on my soul. My burden is heavy. My dreams are beyond control. You don't know me. I want to be a part of your team. You're not better than me. I'd like to ask you some questions. Maybe I'll be a better writer. You have a unique opportunity. You need to build up your child. I trust him with my whole heart. I will not be yours. I will not kiss you. I am not your sweetheart. I said nothing. A deserted island, a lost man, memories of a fatal crash- what's wrong with you? Congratulations, you just committed suicide.

It's time to resign yourself. Facing cancer, your family experienced loss. Increase the signal to noise ratio; we have made it easy to foster a community caring for adults facing cancer. Do you know who can see? I'm sorry you hit your head. It makes your heart pound, your breathing quicken and your forehead sweat. It's that easy. Express your true self. The Southwest Side of Chicago isn't always easy, but taking the time is worth every ounce of effort. As the years teach acceptance and foster empathy, we understand painful fatalism can creep in. The Sox suffer a litany of indignities that are particularly unflattering. Looking for a poem?

Smile! You've got cancer. Cancer is not an illness, it's a gift. The positive thinkers are wrong. The most shocking thing was the extent to which poverty has been criminalized in America. His health review could not be done. I thought adults had silly rules. The inspiration behind cancer features a cluster of holistic poison at the very highest level. It's been a lot of hard work. Thank you for taking the time out of your day. I made it myself.

I'm thrilled to announce the launch of evolving universal humanity to connect and co-create time travel.

I work for you! This physician is currently accepting new patients. Meticulous dissections of depression have set a standard for courage in the face of the mind's adversities, although he never quite achieved the return home. I worked with him for three years. It's amazing how much the *Dies Irae* marks substantial collisions. The reclusive and slightly eccentric mugshot violations experienced toxicity. Final accretion was complicated to some degree by overlap associated with the subsequent arrival.

Citizenship is a component of the diverse illegal entry of people while facilitating legitimate releases. Preservation of historical records will introduce you to availability of federal tax forms. We invite you to visit our landmark building. The world clock shows the current time. Myeloproliferative improvement has been a timeless worldwide favorite experimental metanarrative. Standards are key to the quality of the infrastructure, fueled by exciting reflection. I began to discover a resonance with terminally ill persons. Let your family know that your favorite author used key defensive stops late studying the solar system, sharing the excitement of space exploration with the public. The Red Cross is deeply concerned about the failure of the bride's gorgeous lace gown. You will serve as an integral member of the leadership team. Following in the footsteps of mythology, this book is a blueprint for embedding academic librarians in online environments.

We are proud to announce that we treat fruits and vegetables as a butcher would meat. Thank you to our guests. If you suspect someone is being trafficked, look at what happens at home after the sermon. Intelligent and richly insightful, the story of growing up on the fringes featured shapeshifting depiction of the relationship of child to parent. You have come to the right place! I wanted to share an opportunity for those who may feel drawn to help a young woman with a huge heart. A work that renegotiates the concept of the hypertext to present a reconfigurative narrative moves the right guy. Finally we don't have to sit there. How difficult the experience was! I watched them try professional Tarot consultations and intuitive readings for exceptional healers, leaders, visionaries, and creatives who prefer devotion to the Church. I think I'd like to spoil you. She has trouble staying focused and shifting between tasks, difficulty hiding, and may have inherited a taste for provocation. This is a distraction. She has ventured to take this journey, and now she is lost. Cancer should never have happened. Shadows settle on the place that you left.

I just wanted to apologize, so much that my face hurts. Everything worth loving in this world- life, love, sex, self, God, people, philosophy, politics, comics, art, humor- we hope to find. I'm standing in the middle of a field contemplating the quiet beauty while others scramble to say goodbye. Invisible children love romance. It's very rare for me to read a book, and impossible for me to write one. I love capturing dynamic images of people in their environments. With a new approach that treats the universe as written based on personal experience, you might say that it's more accurate to describe a solution to reality. I've been busy. Sit down with this book. See if you can stop after one page. Last night some crazy shit went down. I am speechless.

A favorite of rich television, I work hard to provide a vital professional spotlight after a journey. Chicago thumbnail fragments have developed in humid forest, and this place was highly recommended. She confronts herself, although never returns home. The people who love historical documents and family trees browse for past auction results. We sit down with the unexpected. This will be the border of the province. The life partner would like to do some minor modification to their decision to let go. It comes as no surprise. He is survived by a daughter, a family.

I had the unique privilege of lived birth, marriage, and death. I am a creative thinker with the ability to create something from nothing. He passed away quietly. Treat yourself like a good friend, practice self-compassion, be reasonable. We got a little taste, but the work wasn't over. It was really early and they came to us due to severe weather conditions. But does it float? We don't keep them going forever.

Death remains a lightning rod. Unfortunately, we forgot to decide. It's not altogether surprising that the creator is taking down the guy. I'm a Messiah and she's my sister. I think I am the complete operative. Cancer doesn't keep the conversation going. I am going to beat the living. This is no small feat. The body won't be able to play. David'd make this weekend epic to make up for my family not coming. The boy veered off the road. I think about that night and I think my life would be tremendously easier if I stayed home. I struggled initially. It's a plea for posthumous life. We want to believe our efforts had meaning. This kid will go far in life- or end up in jail. It has often been this way. The Lord God, who commanded light to shine out of darkness, told reporters "I'd always said it was a long shot." Cancer won't reflect on the life of its creator. Lacking in empathy and prone to violence, we have no idea who's marked for death. It's a fairly generic shape, hard to guess what it is precisely.

The first casualty of every war is the global outpouring of respect. The greatest challenges ask a difficult question. We call these moments Machiavellian because he knew there'd be a whole lot of dead. A dangerous thinker conquered most of the world. The Central Intelligence Agency used American modern art- including rape, abuse and incest. The best way to read this e-book is on a tablet-style device. They had something within their power that they could use, and it could only be used if they understood the policy on containment. We're sorry to hear. I write books. If you've been paying attention, there is no evidence of unauthorized activity of any kind.

Take time to read a collection of poems. Writers sometimes confuse the paradox. Didn't we hear about our dad in violation of law? I remember thinking that unsteady mood and rising catch variability reported odd glowing and mysterious flickers of light. Now the phenomenon may finally be related to death. What exactly are the rules? Dielectric splitting of nanoscale disks was studied experimentally and via finite-difference time-domain simulations through systematic uncoating. This was his sick way. Learn to let go and create a life you love with the high-speed crash. He didn't do a very good job. His father had died. It does not take much to summon the rage that consumed him. Poetry could be solved using a regular expression with negative lookbehind, which is experimentally supported in grep as pointed out by the Illinois state trooper. It came as a rude shock.

We didn't find that. You can try slavery with our hands. We work at a distance trying to measure what is going on, rather than figuring out why communications are breaking down. We'll find out what happened. Few words are required. Now the question is whether parenthetical citation involves coverage this deep. Do you know how you want to die? That's exactly why it's so appealing. It is a great pleasure.

The cessation of all phenomena, eternal oblivion, is a friendly reminder that life is slipping away. Unquestionably, are we in some sense immortal? Would immortality be desirable? If there is one thing we can be certain of, it's that we will die. What does it mean to die? There are only two things you can count on in life. I'm not afraid; I just don't want to be there when it happens. We still can't quite believe. Who can look at the dark, skeletal figure on Card 13 and not feel uneasy? Here we see the face of our deepest fear. You are not going to die. You might think you are, but you will be missed eternally. Here is our humble tribute to you. We still can't wrap our heads around the fact that you are gone. We're here to set the record straight. What are the final weeks, days and very moments of life really like? A yielding up of the breath or spirit? A return to our original dust?

You do not have any means of growing. I recently crave for better themes. I can help. Explore the beautiful creative security. You're protected. Why start from scratch? I'm so pleased to have found an intuitive system featuring a flawless Occam's razor. Just about everyone seems so close to being helpful but yet always off. Bullying may have lasting effects on kids. Our mission is to make meaningful connections. Let's get it done. The asteroid was not a threat, your trusted friend in this world.

We're calling this crazy, uncensored, no-holds-barred show the heavy heart. All windshield wipers on all cars worked at just one or two speeds. We provide a respectful and supportive killing. If you want to know my reasons, you will need to sacrifice. Yet another banker has committed suicide. The first four sentences are interesting; the fifth blew my mind. He was also a cook. Why don't you stand over there? Had we but world enough, and time, this coyness, lady, were no crime. What else can I do to help? As my father suffered, I angrily languished in the corners, an exile. Everyone needs a little magic. Police did recover a weapon. When I came to realize that this truly happened, I felt sad because I guess I was wrong. No one can take us out. You are precious in my sight, you are beautiful, and I love you. You'll die.

For beginners in the spiritual life, the greatest obstacle can be a false standard of perfection. I had a talk with my daughter. There's been some activities in my house I haven't been completely aware. So this is how it all started. I might want you to die a painful death. I'm entirely serious. Many people feel ashamed at the idea. What is it like to find out that the man you thought was your dad is heartbreaking? If you had lived, we would all be miserable, you and your children. Each one shall be put to death for his own abusive, violent family. The mission is to strengthen families and build communities. I have failed. I wish I could just escape all of this.

After a homorganic consonant, unstressed circuit speech connects the oceans. It plays several distinct roles within habitats for the continuing benefit of Homeland Security. It performs, facilitating legitimate trade, which will introduce you to music by the Institute of Electrical Substance Abuse. The execution of his constitutional liberties features exhibition galleries, each displaying major artifacts from MFA programs. Criticism debate in literature is a grassroots nonprofit organization dedicated to the Pacific. Responsibility for space protocol parameter system management is no evidence that general aviation pilots are dedicated to hospice. The agency that is principally responsible for advising the President on conditioning provides free analysis on the social collaborative effort to restore health. Join us to discuss the book.

Widely used in pathfinding and graph traversal, the process of plotting heuristic use in baseball explores the design, development, and meaning of hybrid atom-photon quantum ballet through the eyes of children. Today we're teaming up to share simple but fully customizable art. You can choose, stuff, stitch, fluff and dress your new furry friend. We are very pleased to announce the solution. Tune in to hear about the future dynasty. Worried? Significant progress would allow fundamental advances in all areas of planetary resources. 1 in 4 children don't know where their next meal is coming from. One of the really good things is that the work you put in often leads you to stuff you didn't know about. There is no longer any need for the dream. Your family may not be together when disaster strikes. Any person could share with anyone else, anywhere. I thought I'd look. I'd have never had the balls to publish my first book. Settle the score once and for all.

The best psychological drama has been working hard during the last years to earn the reputation of being a crisis. Their children navigate their lives. The devastating impact that cancer has is violence in the family. Have you ever wondered what goes on behind the scenes? Nevertheless, intellectual fugitive waves always want you to indulge when it comes to life. I believe so deeply in the life-saving work to end domestic violence, so that all relationships can embrace the principles of respect, strength, self-love and divine femininity. We want to do something special, something totally different. We're not gonna take it. Great joy was among the first to identify the evils of human trafficking. What did I get myself into? There is nothing in the world more beautiful. It is the still ecstasy of nature. It's a mystery. Couples gone wrong must be enabled. What more could anyone ask for?

I've planned in exacting detail. I've left things until the last minute. I've spent thousands on the most neglected peace as a father and a man, both ordinary and extraordinary. I have a journal. The way people live, you're in the right place. Deception seemed bleak. I can dance if I want to. I was raised in these dusty repositories. I have been involved. I hope you will join me. I have gotten the chance on many occasions. I doubt death around the world right now. Surviving it is a hard test. It started, like most disasters, with a sense of triumph. His dying wish is shaping up to be a titanic clash, with pugilistic litigants trading charges and sorry-looking hair. It's finally here.

The tree from the front yard is gone, apparently. The exterior of the house looks very different now; I remember it being darker somehow. Let's be unreasonable. Spring arrives one month from today. I felt so horrible this past January. I hated every minute of it. But with two weeks of sun, fresh air, and a new perspective, I feel like a million bucks. I honestly loved this book. It had to happen. I tried it. You need not be sorry for her. I take my job seriously. It was a long time ago. I have almost forgotten my dream. The city kids will just never understand. This year isn't much different. His death was tragic.

His last chance to understand, believe, an old man finally fulfills his lifelong dream without love. A lifetime challenge notable for being the end of cancer begins to accelerate the pace. One is all you need. If you've found yourself, you're brand new. When children are properly nourished they can grow to be healthy and productive. We can't accept any more sarcasm. Just by speaking about it, you can stop. Imagine what it must be like waking 673 million kilometres from anywhere. This NOVA report examines the science and politics of love, including politics, economics, planning and design, history and entertainment. For those who don't just take it for granted, the common answer is that Europeans made the maps. More than 60,000 young children end in emergency departments every year because they got into medicines while their parent or caregiver was not looking. Homeless or thinking of running away? We apologize for the inconvenience. Can you explain hard anger? The universe is a hologram. I guess you realise I'm going to grind through the accelerator. We don't expect to be violent. Paul said he has no intention of going anywhere.

Quality is everything. You are here. Write to the Help Desk. Sometimes little apparent force can fit your needs. Arriving early at the supremacy we think about transformational influence on political physics. Incredible opportunities to change the past reflect inspiring hands against over-exploitation. If you're having issues, we introduce to you a catalyst for change. I am Shakespeare. A strange sign of the times, but even more alarming is the scientific consensus on climate change and its worsening impacts. Solely published abroad, without compliance with formalities, his merciless mother explains how important cross-examination is, and describes his first time cross-examining a witness. Men wearing what appear to be government uniforms fired at unseen targets with automatic rifles.

Early goals proved to be insurmountable. All buses are currently running on time. We hope you find what you are looking for. The city was incorporated in 1970. The city is four square miles. They rarely had relatives. It's "couldn't care less," just in case you've been saying "could care less," which makes no sense. Find homes for sale in Illinois. It was a great day filled with impressive renovations over the years. With a transparent and informative process, you can relax knowing that he has responded to six robberies or attempted robberies of local businesses. There were no reported searches. Death is located in the heart of every child. How the hell did he ever become a doctor? In a city with as much star power, it's only natural. What are you waiting for?

Severe storms including tornadoes struck late afternoon, knocking out power, damaging buildings and spawning floods. Hear directly from farmers. Gas may smell funny, but it's no joke. Call us to report a leak. Anything's possible. It is often noted as a microcosm of the entire country. The dear leader liked to look at things. The Central Chapter helps disaster victims, teaches

CPR/First Aid, trains children to live safer and supports military in 8 counties. We give voice to a creative state. Romeoville is the property of the Secretary of State. It is every doctor's professional responsibility to support the government. Joliet is your source for concealed carry applications. As Will County Executive, I am proud to welcome you to one of the fastest growing counties in the United States. I didn't exactly get the full ambiance here since there are too many inmates, not enough cells and quick action in Chicago is no small feat. He saw a giant crow flying overhead, cawing. A line of storms blew through Thursday evening, bringing with it a brief rise in temperatures, which were quickly replaced with strong wind gusts and consumer complaints, revealing residents are increasingly worried over how revealing entertainment in Springfield is.

Toxic grammatically coordinate words promote disability. It performs many releases to ensure prevention of creating, developing, integrating. Severed formal ties enjoy resolution of all the work during a lull in the fighting. Investigative grassroots domain management is also available. Misinformation will tell terminally ill persons we can enjoy life. Endure the tribulations of childhood, building a scientific understanding of the mind to reduce suffering and promote well-being. No brilliant thoughts. You try your first sentence but it's awful. Winter will make a harsh return much of the eastern United States next week.

One could vaguely construe that your own body as experienced by yourself, as yourself. Your own body manifests itself to you mainly as possibilities of fission products. Radioactive materials have always a few days to a few decades to reconnect after release from death row. Boundaries have been set, and you built a wall. Not all died that night. Ask anyone. It's your story. How are you telling and preserving it? Do you have a clear vision? I hope you enjoy it. No, you are not dreaming! I had been preached to, analyzed, cursed, and counseled, but no one had ever said 'I identify with what's going on with you.' It's been said that you make all your mistakes during your 20s. It's been snowing almost every other day. I think he would have. Hopefully taking the first step out of your cocoon will lead you toward your dreams. I am fortunate and grateful. So did you. See if you can find it.

Chicago tells the epic story of race against advice. The man responsible was found dead today. The highly anticipated announcement is an essential milestone. One can always find like-minded people to develop a critical eye. Let me know if you see anything. Thank you for understanding. Forgotten U.S. President Chester A. Arthur is more historically significant than Radiohead. The truth is that humans are good at a lot of things, but time is not one of them. It's not our fault. The war resembles appalling conditions with magnitude larger than 5. This hurricane was the deadliest weather disaster. Storm tides of 8 to 15 ft inundated the whole of Galveston Island, as macroscopic processes appear to be temporally directed. Systems spontaneously evolve to future equilibrium states, but they still probably thought of a similar set of actions. We used longitudinal statistical models to examine whether some of the fanfare has died down. The only reason that was never the plan was because I never thought that I'd ever be able to make a living writing. I know it could be worse. I took my degree of Doctor of Medicine. If you have cancer, an understanding of perception can significantly improve both love and charity. Okay,

I'm calling it. Over time it's become particular: I may have shape-shifted by the digital moonlight. I'm the first male member of my family in three generations never to have the death knell for all things righteous. No, they shouldn't. At first glance the decision depends on the preferences of a land ravaged by pandas. Tsunami waves are radiating outward after a magnitude 9 earthquake. There's not much left to say except that I'm really glad I see nothing to which I could take exception. He was dead. My body is running cold at the thought of it.

Always green, we regret that out of necessity we have a guilty secret, always relevant if you need to see a doctor. We urge you to make safety of your child when it all started. Many thought you are old. You can still navigate, but it will not support blazing through the melodic hardcore theology. We are experienced. We are dependable. We are safe. We are excited to share all the wonderful things happening.

Families with children are the only reasons I go anymore. I prefer to hermit in the scenic, hilly woodlands. Cancer isn't just a job. Would rats choose to take drugs if given a stimulating environment and company? Charlie is an indie web developer and family man. He lives in Virginia. You should grab a beer with him. It's a second chance. It can be in its natural or semi-natural state, or planted, and is set aside for human enjoyment or for the Amber Alert system. Though generations have come and gone, Fenway remains, much like it did the day it opened on April 20, 1912. We invite you to take in a roller coaster. How do physics laws affect ride design? The rolling foothills are filled with a variety of wildlife, nestled in the Blue Ridge Mountains, just beyond the energy of downtown Asheville. Register for the Broad Street Run and raise money for the the team behind the popular Marlowe Restaurant. Socrates is happy to announce that, after a competitive search process, the World Trade Center is dedicated to restoring and bringing back to life a dynamic metropolitan oasis in a city happily inundated with summertime recreation, picnics or enjoying a beautiful day at Chimney Rock. View the kinetic energy, potential energy and friction as all it is supposed to be- fun, fulfilling and full of surprises! Dare to tackle the most intense rides. What happened this week? Those were the days. The Trojans were no match for events. Something wonderful is going to happen. Change is coming; watch for it.

The polymorphism is associated with susceptibility to rheumatoid arthritis in Champaign. They're using health management systems to make their cases effectively. Children of incarcerated parents were here. Simplify your taxes during the Joint Hearings on Tax and Incentives Protection. We stand committed to reducing the number of fatalities to zero. Welcome to the City of Chicago. All persons who wish to file any sort of application with the Board must first create personal art. Dispute resolution users please be advised that the information contained in this database is the property of the the US Senate. Last night, we held our second forum and hosted an enthusiastic group. What a forecast! Bloomington-Normal has everything you need and more.

Something will happen. Up to the time that or when; they did not come. There was widespread anger, leading to the abandoned antonyms and definitions. The end of the world may be hacked. Wow, what a book! I think I was crying with a refreshingly unique and quirky edge. A brain-dead pregnant woman lies on a hospital bed no longer deprived of life, even if that means the violence stops. I needed to tell them and I didn't want them finding out on Instagram. I wanted national outrage. Stay as long or as short as you'd like. In this section you'll find an innovative, highly entertaining and suspenseful thriller. You're not welcome here. Do something about it. Most of what you know about zombies makes no sense. Keep watching. In 1987, Andre Sarano took a photograph of Christ on the cross in a jar of urine. The result is he is dead. We had no idea. I was five years old. Everyone charged with a penal offence has the right to be presumed innocent. The only dream worth having is to dream that you will live while you are alive and die only when you are dead. You're not going to fly with your kid. What if you could know the exact moment of your death? He's serious. I wish there was only today, just right now, and no forever.

A surprise development that breaks from tradition, most won't be returning home. But before you start panicking, a series of books about managing the psychological effects help you live a more balanced and happy life. It's time to make a few decisions. You probably didn't like the news. Go to bed, call it a day. Avoid being at the center of attention. Look at your strengths, weaknesses, opportunities and challenges. His body has begun to betray him to the point that these strategies can make the thrill ride scary. There are some new developments. I want to grow as an artist, and I'm taking a step. Is it a joke? Depends on how I feel. He was wrong.

I stopped after eight years, determined to give up. When you breathe, you can get lung cancer. I think it's way past time. If you need know-how, we're here for you. No question is too big or too small. The place where someone participates in a particular way to die is unavailable. This is where cancer begins. You must be a U.S. citizen. In most states, you must be 18 years old, but some states do allow 17 year olds. It is taking longer than expected. Quitting smoking is not easy, but you can do it. These key questions are once again being brought in room-size metal boxes secure against electromagnetic leaks.

Witness the rebirth of seriously ill children and their literacy skills, empowering them as a catalyst for revitalization. We are privileged to serve a unique position, owing to its geographical position on the fairgrounds. Come alive to the relics of St. Cuthbert and the Venerable Bede. Relationships built on honesty are the foundation of who we are. I can't wait to read whatever he writes next. Leave a message and someone will call back within 24 hours. Road crews and emergency responders spent Thursday moving abandoned cars. Tobacco offers many benefits! Why? Your willingness was evident. The attention to detail and your efforts to work were obvious. Join us in the great human race. Please upgrade your flash. Who are we? Please join in its mission to end domestic and sexual violence. You're searching. The public is always invited. Where's the love?

The shuttered power leaked toxic sludge. Specializing in medicine, a new version is available. You should use it. The Medical Board exists to regulate medicine and surgery for the benefit and protection of the people. You will find information here for those we serve. I wasn't home and some snow knocked out the power and my turtle froze to death. I used a blow dryer and a sock to revive him. Your financial contributions are critical to our program. A raw sewage spill near Burlington has been completely overhauled and new standards are to be implemented. Asheville can offer an experience any way you like it. Income inequality has become a central part of Tar Heel sports. We work to protect the public's right to know. No wetlands, no seafood. I determined my recently completed painting needed transforming science. Church planting reaches many ethnic groups with the gospel, as well as many unchurched communities and unreached population segments. Learn how to protect yourself. We create hope for parents. If there is any conflict, then one simple way to support the morale, health and human services, and recreational needs of every child is not available because of Duke Energy's coal ash spill. As a nation, our diversity is our greatest strength. You are finely tuned artists who bring passion and personality to every performance. Four students' lunch at the F. W. Woolworth Building would empower activists; we've got some ideas on what those changes should bring together: all the people involved in a young child's life. Whenever you feel an impulse to perpetrate a piece of exceptionally fine writing, obey it- whole-heartedly.

Solely abroad, without cross-examination, I'd tried. Supportive oncology consumes you. You are the best! How did you like the medical treatment? Suggestions are provided for responsible force reduction. Incurable disease is a hoax. Chances are good that any problems you have are big ones, and the easy ones have already been solved. It is the third largest city and has a varied climate- very cold winter, hot summer. America can take a

clear stand without intervening. Authorities were biased and con-
centrated too much on the psoriasis. Part of his job is to know
what is going on. We will interact with them through writing
about the errors that I have seen most frequently. Chicago White
Sox centerfielder Alejandro De Aza touts a healthy lifestyle with
extensive job listings provided by the *LA Times* Business section.
Search a pile of my own dirty laundry which I set on the couch for
"just a second." This is me after I finished the book. The spans of
time, the debilitating decisions made by cheap Viagra- that was
never the plan. Lead can be toxic. You should probably stop.
Why? The horrible truth about what really happens during the
revolution is a vital interface between global policies. I don't know
your name. Curse the crying children. I have a large enough col-
lection now that I can pick and choose. Life is not happy.

Make it yours. Our understanding of the universe has
changed dramatically. An American astronaut is sent on a joint
U.S.-Soviet space mission. The National Hurricane Center's Tropi-
cal Cyclone Reports contain comprehensive information from both
sides of the Atlantic on the move to make data more open and free.
Thanks, y'all. Nearly three quarters of the 178 countries in the in-
dex score below five, on a scale from 10 to 0. Common vulnerabili-
ties must plan to maintain recent additions to the ground forces
for the foreseeable future. Palladium-catalyzed cross couplings in
organic components of our water footprint support a healthy New
Jersey. Most research in data mining and knowledge discovery re-
lies heavily on the availability of data sets. That is why jobs must
be our number one focus. The true engine is a county-by-county
enumeration of religious bodies, delighted to invite you to submit

your original and innovative work to the first ever pervasive disease.

You can make a difference! The truth wears off. Is there something wrong? A total eclipse of the Moon occurs during the early morning hours. It's time to stop being scared.

Intelligent assistance and high-performance special needs of offices in 23 countries dates back more than 150 years. I believe that if imaging and preservation did not exist, the future would be bleak indeed. We treat you with respect. Fill in the fields and hit submit. Thanks for your interest. We make art. Intangible objectives integrating external applications experience relief. You're seeking to improve the quality and availability of alcohol, and to find a home for every child in need. Poetry and novels help you become healthy and self-sufficient. The United States Congress is aware. It's never too late to foster care and family permanence. We definitely encourage students to complete at least one before they graduate. Use at your own risk.

Ten years to plan for their newborn daughter's future sounds like a naïve question given the violent predictions. Ask a lawyer. When you are older, inevitable events happen. Determination, strength of character, resolve deliberately exerted to restrain one's own impulses. Writing can be as simple as typing. After your death, if you understood Catholic philosophy, you can turn on here. I am proud to welcome you. Do you like to listen to music while you work? He was more than just a boy. I just don't think people have enough access to my opinions. They give you answers that make them feel better about themselves, not necessarily what they truly think. Get real. It is difficult to think. There are many ways to take action. Activism is not terrorism. I'm thrilled to change the world with every initiative. I'm not a doctor and I never played one on TV. I'm not a fan of being called praiseworthy. What is it to act freely? Most of us don't recognize just how far the things go. Men are obsolete. I could have chosen to do something else. Ultimately, it comes back to this: I have no idea.

Who is staying? I was there dressed as a pirate. Any chance you've still got it for me? Real-time flight information (arrivals and departures) is impacted by several types of hazards during a lifetime. Americans also travel more than ever before to the Red Planet. Join forces to launch the strange monument built for universal mindfulness. Mindfulness helps people change the way they think, feel and act. Four whole days of the very best disaster preparedness, providing an objective base for vulnerability assessment, requires all parties to be ready together. Discover the latest earthquake- the dynamics of conflict, violence and development. Thinking ahead, plastics are too valuable to throw away. We transmit high voltage electricity from generators to distribution systems, which in turn deliver it to the consumer. They understand how he earned it. Nearly all tobacco use begins during youth and young adulthood. Following the death, stay in touch. We've proven by reductio ad absurdum that one or both of the principles we began with is false. The real question is: do we let ourselves choose to grow? There are cooler ideas out there. Everyone looking for justice must consist of a variety of small preparations, also to share. We still lack a decent gateway, because we are passionate people. Don't display this message again. You may want to get educated and take a few basic steps.

Introverted, self-contained, withdrawn from life, the past affecting trust. The knife wasn't for the Iraqis. What is the difference? Help bridge the gap between the actual cost of your education and the limited support of internal revenue. Some believe that it lacks misunderstanding. Anyone can view your profile. I believe in you. There's no need to listen. Your sound control and critical analysis building a friendly environment, including reliable rules, do not disadvantage us. Families preserve and protect shutdown growth. Enjoy your moment. I am your partner for life. When we search our thoughts, you have a right to enjoy the success they have achieved. If you are interested, please enjoy this short film featuring a wonderful unique experience to help you bring about improvements.

One of the few official statements about current issues works to find countless fun. Get us. Russian troops are already there under an interstate agreement about a military base. If you want a family, let your opinion be heard. We first heard last June. It still isn't ready. They were sentenced for murder. Don't think. Increasingly alone, it was a descent into chaos. I never thought I'd be able to make a living. Dress conservatively. It's not our fault. I know it could be worse. Cancer took my toxic donors. But not far away- I'm calling it. No, they shouldn't. Most never made it. One of the things that I occasionally have to deal with is conflict between God and obsolete ancient principles. We know that it will be possible to search reflections of a basic distrust of memory. Tamoxifen asked a good question yesterday about the most prominent myths. A strong background is necessary for success. Dad, I know your life is not happy. One of the things I've been hoping is every conflict were not yet come into force. My body is running cold at the thought of it. I am such a wuss.

I specialize in unavailability. This initiative proposes expanded use of instruments, resulting in a nice gift. He gave us an IOU. The love of my life also happens to be putting it off til later. Another option that may be available to you is flowers. We provide the wedding gown of your dreams! We have served an offender charged with a criminal offense, including but not limited to a violation of horrible experiences. I am so excited to write this. My weapon of choice brought kaizen, a Japanese word meaning "continuous improvement," to the avoidance of time consuming proceedings. In this approach, I need to escape. If other options haven't worked out and you're open to the idea, the best option remains a big secret. I have a feeling that it's going to be a great one, but this is beginning to change. Things are getting real serious. No version of the system ever quite withstood the test of additional refined observations. I'm not the kind of person who will buy the cheaper version. Do you need help to walk away? You pay by the length of your ride, so you also have to put your ticket in to exit. If you jumped in, you'll have to jump out too. Just want it over with?

If you are in contact with medicine, they have entered into a comprehensive settlement. Every baby deserves throwaway lives. Pointing lasers at aircraft, illustrating major achievements in painting, sculpture, and graphic arts, traces its origins to 1743. It concluded on Sunday, as hundreds cheered. The best live music in the world works to ensure that all people have clean air and energy, as well as safe and sufficient food. We are your family. Across primary visual cortex, neurons that respond preferentially to stimuli are clustered in so-called orientation domains. A child's heart helps surgeons save life. We use science to understand the world.

Your home is the place for quality you can trust. It has been more than a decade. After falling out of favor for many years, lost art is enjoying a revival. Dismissed as a rip-off of the White Sox offense, we've spent all season being pumped about the eternal seductiveness of life. A reproductive structure in angiosperms, often conspicuously colourful, Philadelphia is a catalyst. I really appreciate you appreciating my vision, and using your clear talents to bring that vision to life. It's about life, friendship and defining yourself on your own terms. Take a deep breath; you're finally in the right place. I admire the work. Let's face it, today's world can be a little overwhelming. So many details to take care of and decisions to make.

Specifying or particularizing, as opposed to indefinite or generalizing, control leaves untouched art and culture. Its mission is to offer peace and tranquility as he declared control. Many said President Obama's stern warning on Friday was inadequate. A man waved your inside source. It is home to a diverse group. Our efforts are driven by redneck innovation. Neuroscientists are automating neural imaging and recording. They save children's lives and help them reach their full potential. I think I have a solution. You and I were cut. It's not good. We cannot allow these leaders to carry on with their tricks. For more than 40 years, we used to wait. Unidentified gunmen wearing camouflage uniforms guard creative thinking- a truly radical idea. One theory of everything, which eluded even Einstein, gets a niche market. They weren't welcome, but they weren't leaving. Tea Party propaganda said it was trash.

A fundamental social group in society typically consisting of one or two parents and their children, who share goals and values, have heart and soul. You love your town. Work together. Use fluoride toothpaste. Nuclear action directed by a notorious mafia clan provides answers. Many people still succeed though they come from less-than-ideal situations, but having our basic needs met, knowing that our parents love us was cut off. The truth is that we are now separate and unequal. They insist they are related. The invisibility cloak needs new batteries. I want our children to go to schools worthy of their potential. You know what feels right. It is important to plan in advance. I can't believe this just happened! He depends on me. We can help you make it. It is not an accident.

Eager to get started? Demanding authority connects people with friends and others who work, study and live around them. People use excellent infinitive reconsideration. It's performing more poorly than it once did. These principles describe how we deal with freedom. Please wait. Describe the information you want, and the striving to bring the best experience welcomes you. Could you please pass me the salt? Look at the possible responses and choose the best. We'll need a car seat. Permission can be granted free of charge. All settings are optional. There are several things you should know. We sincerely value your comments and read every message you send us. While we would like to respond, it is not possible to do so. Philadelphia is a gem. If it is obvious vandalism, drive behavior through the full stack, including routing chronological religious obligations, from removing an abandoned vehicle to reporting New Jersey is responsible. It's not easy being at the mercy of someone who asks the inappropriate.

We ask you the questions and you give us the answers. After all validations are done you will provide critical mental health services. One account is all you need. This is a story about how actions have consequences, no matter how just or moral you think your cause happens to be. It isn't a reality yet. We had a little chat. From the moment it begins beating until the moment it stops, the human heart works tirelessly. To do no evil, to cultivate good, to purify one's mind: this is the teaching of the Buddhas. Got questions? There will be a difference, but it sure is a lot of fun trying to crack the code. It doesn't have to be. I am bored. If you're like most people, you've been going to physicians ever since you were born, but you're unaware that some or all of them could know very little. Consequently, you got crushed. She left? I'll see you there. Ask me anything. In about 1981, I read quantum physics and parapsychology in The Journal of the American Society for Psychical Instruments. Reproduction of this information with alteration is unfair and deceptive. I didn't want to post about this, because frankly, it is exhausting.

Do you know freedom? All of the stories of hope and inspiration facilitate life. It was established through the individual's contribution to collaborative links with exceptional accomplishment. An exceptional career made distinctive contributions. Stay away. Just a misunderstanding. We went there solely for you so you can unsubscribe. Allegations of bullying and hazing continue. Education is the most important long-term investment we can make in our future. Cancer reflects the diversity of energies and lingering backlash. Profound interest and significant contributions conferred tradition recognized by life and memory of a relative.

Do you want to do a good deed? Are you interested in change? Don't let these myths confuse you. Many may never get the call. They may not know how living works, and they may be surprised. Thank you. I'd like to talk to someone. In response to the shortage, relatives, loved ones, friends and even individuals with no prior relationship are serving. There is no minimal amount. End suffering. The thought of being able to help save three people's lives every time I go makes me not generally tax deductible. Children need your help now. It's more difficult so you get the get the most from your embryos. The human mission to Mars is lifesaving for homeless and low income men, women, and youth living with and affected by HIV and AIDS. Join the fight against cancer. You can honor or remember loved ones against cancer. It's the ultimate win-win. You are giving a precious gift. It is what we do.

This is unavailable. You acknowledge that you have read and agree. Take action now. What will happen? Cancer begins quickly, facilitating an all-hands-on-deck approach. That's the core of the solution. I hope that enough support brings importance. You can get lung cancer. In fact, you can do it with your friends. It's quite powerful. It is taking longer than expected. You must be registered. Quitting smoking is not easy. We're here for you. It is a product of its times. He did expect this question.

A journey that spans billions of years is private, nondenominational, culturally rich and ethnically diverse. I am unable to work because of mental anguish. Interim Prime Minister Arseniy Yatseniuk urges Putin to pull back his troops. Russia's move brought a warning from Ukraine against further incursions. What were freely related aims capture screaming big ideas from an unbiased and thought-provoking perspective. We cannot allow these leaders to carry on with their tricks. Each day a different image or photograph of our fascinating universe is featured. Make a difference. Explore life. Now it's time to go. Do they wish to see unity and dynamism? A disease is threatening. This morning, I see that some people are quite abuzz about spring. I'm committed. A quick note before we start: it's our issue. I will come forth as gold. It's your world. It's coming.

Death is an extensive international and domestic network, uniting the deadly consequences for those affected by cancer spreading. Make efforts towards clean air and smokefree living, as lung cancer produced aggressive growth. Family needs optimal and ethical protection. Death is the oldest and largest single life activity. Suicide sets ethical standards. Cancer promotes discipline. We are the solution.

The causes are diverse, complex, and only partially understood. Many things are known to increase the risk. As the war rages on, adult survivors take great pleasure when it metastasizes, spreading to other organs or the bones. Early detection is based on theory. New drugs could extend patients' lives by days at a cost of thousands and thousands of dollars, prompting some doctors to refuse to use them. Is it any wonder that the disease has become a gold mine for profiteers? Consult a doctor if you have uncontrolled growth of abnormal cells in the body. That's why we're here. We have been fighting for decades. You can beat this. It can affect almost any part of the body. Normal cells multiply when the body needs them, and die when the body doesn't need them. Who would guess? Tracking evolution may reveal the key mutations. Genetic diversity is a major challenge in the era of personalised medicine. It has turned out to be tougher to crack than everyone hoped. Someone I know was diagnosed. Philadelphia never shies away from demanding the necessary but hard changes. Are you at risk? It sucks. Sometimes it's hard to look forward when you think your entire life is moving backwards. We're breaking barriers. If the devil can't defeat me, pray for sick children who face this horrible disease. It can often be treated and cured. During this time, you may experience some disruption. We will, of course, aim to keep this slaughterhouse accused of selling meat from cows. Please feel free to read.

Living together in drugs, crime, and other dangers to the general public, having shared violence through persistent relations, cancer spreading. Thirty years ago, the old deal that held us together started to unwind. Was it an inevitable process? It's a mystery to me. Maintain constant vigilance. Women who meet for tea wearing red hats and purple dresses help the world breathe. The semi-finalists for crew selection for the Mars Arctic mission have been announced. Applied mathematics, in partnership with computational science, is essential in solving many real-world problems. Our mission is to build paranormal congresses, clinical practice guidelines, and the nation through art and history exhibitions. Is your backpack stuffed with lunar samples? Tomorrow is built today. We appreciate your patience during this exciting transition, and we will respond.

ACKNOWLEDGEMENTS

I would like to thank Therese Pope, Karren Aleiner, Nicola Quinn, and T. de los Reyes for their encouragement and friendship, and for reviewing several sections of the draft as it was in progress.

Thanks also to Kenneth Goldsmith, for his kind words and condolences, as well as for championing conceptual, uncreative writing which formed the backbone of this book.

I am especially grateful for the friendship, mentorship, and encouragement of Al Filreis. You taught me what I know of writing and poetry, and your enthusiasm about the idea for this book in the days following my father's death gave much needed encouragement to proceed. I simply could not done this work without your teaching and encouragement.

Thanks also to Peggy Haymes, Sandy Gentei Stewart, Roz Leiser, and Nancy Mullins, for helping me find my way out of the fog.

Thank you to my daughters Hayley and Melanie, who inspire me to be the best father I can be, and who lovingly forgive my shortcomings.

I am very grateful to my wife Pamela, who understood my need to do this work. Your love and encouragement was essential. I don't know how I got so lucky, and I love you very much.

Finally, I want to thank my father. Dad, I get it. I understand. I can still remember times when you tried and hadn't yet given up. I forgive you.

Mark Snyder grew up in Evergreen Park, Illinois. He serves as a Community TA in the course in Modern and Contemporary American Poetry at Coursera.org under Prof. Al Filreis. He has created two albums of experimental music- *Necessary Evil* and *Requiem*- the latter a secular conceptual setting of the Mass composed in the days immediately prior to the death of his father. He lives in rural North Carolina and practices general community psychiatry. He lives with his wife and daughters.